GU01217778

QUESTIONS
in STANDARD GRADE
COMPUTING STUDIES

Arlen Pardoe
and
Kevin Thompson

Published by
Leckie & Leckie
8 Whitehill Terrace
St. Andrews
Scotland KY16 8RN
Tel. 01334 475656
Fax. 01334 477392
email: s.leckie@leckie-and-leckie.co.uk
web: www.leckie-and-leckie.co.uk

Edited by
Neil Kennedy

Thanks also to
Bruce Ryan, Hamish Sanderson and Fiona McNee

ISBN 1-898890-45-5

A CIP Catalogue record is available from the British Library.

Printed in Scotland by Inglis Allen on environmentally-friendly paper. The paper is made from a mixture of sawmill waste, forest thinnings and wood from sustainable forests.

Leckie & Leckie

Contents

1. Introduction

1. Standard Grade Computing Studies

There are three main areas of study:

- Knowledge and understanding of computing facts
- Problem solving in computing situations
- Practical assessment

2. What these Questions cover

These questions test the Knowledge and Understanding that you need to know for Foundation, General and Credit level. It is impossible to test absolutely everything but you will find that the main topics have questions associated with them.

To help you in your revision, the questions for Foundation and General level are in normal type (like this).

The extra Credit level questions are in italics (like this) on a shaded background. Your teacher will tell you whether you need to try the Credit level questions.

3. Revision Notes

We strongly recommend that you obtain a copy of 'Standard Grade Computing Studies Revision Notes' published by Leckie & Leckie. The questions in this book are based on the information in the Revision Notes. Reading the Revision Notes first will help you answer the questions.

4. How to use the questions

These questions are written to help you with the revision of the Knowledge and Understanding section of your course.

There are several ways in which these questions can be used:

- as homework exercises to help you as you study each section in your course
- as you complete each section during your Standard Grade course
- as part of your final revision when you are getting close to your Standard Grade examination.

Which method you choose depends on what best suits your circumstances.

5. Answers

Specimen answers are provided for each of the questions.

These are in the pull-out centre section of this book. You are advised to take them out and put them away where you are not tempted to peek at them when attempting the questions.

To pull out the Answers section, remove the centre staple.

If this book has been provided by your school, then your teacher will probably have removed the Answers section before issuing you with it.

Although specimen answers to the questions are given in this book, it is only your teacher who can tell you if **your** answer is good enough.

2. Computer Applications

General Purpose Packages

System Requirements

1. A modern computer system is used to run General Purpose Packages. Suggest typical requirements for:

   a) the speed of the Central Processing Unit;

   b) the backing storage devices used;

   c) the other peripheral devices attached to the Central Processing Unit.

2. Briefly describe the following types of computer:

   a) a desktop computer

   b) a laptop computer

   c) a palmtop computer.

3. a) Give **two** reasons why a floppy disc drive might be needed on a computer system running a <u>General Purpose Package</u>.

   b) Give **three** reasons why a user might prefer to use a laser or an inkjet printer instead of a dot-matrix printer.

4. *a) What is an **Expert System** (also called a **Knowledge System**)?*

   *b) Name **two** areas covered by Knowledge Systems and give the occupations of people who would use them in that way.*

See page 4 of 'Standard Grade Revision Notes'

Storage

5. Name **three** different types of data which can be stored in General Purpose Packages and give one example for each type.

6. a) What name is given to the process of regularly making a copy of the data produced by a General Purpose Package?

   b) Explain why it is important to make a copy of your data in this way.

7. *Give a typical storage capacity for each of the following backing storage devices:*

   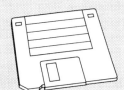

   a)   5.25" floppy disc
   b)   3.5" floppy disc
   c)   fixed hard disc
   d)   CD-ROM

Need for GPPs

8. In the 1980s a range of software tools called <u>General Purpose Packages</u> were developed to help people with common computing tasks.

   Describe **three** tasks which people wanted to be done by a computer.

9. *Briefly describe what is done by each of the following General Purpose Packages:*

   a)   a database;
   b)   a word-processor;
   c)   a spreadsheet.

   Name the extra hardware and software which would be needed, other than that normally associated with General Purpose Packages, to send the information electronically from one office to another.

See pages 5 and 6 of 'Standard Grade Revision Notes'

Common Features

10. A number of processes can be carried out by <u>all</u> General Purpose Packages.

    One process to do with handling documents is <u>starting up a new document</u>. This begins a new document of the application with no data entered.

    Explain what happens in each of the following processes:

    a)   Open

    b)   Print part

    c)   Amend data

    d)   Copy data

    e)   Move data

---

11. A process that is common to textual data in all General Purpose Packages is to <u>change the appearance</u> of the text.

    Describe some of the features of text that can be changed in this way.

---

12. *Describe the purpose of a <u>printer driver</u>.*

---

13. *Explain the terms <u>header</u> and <u>footer</u> and give an example of the sort of data which they might contain.*

---

14. a) *Explain the term <u>Human Computer Interface</u>.*

    b) *Name **two** examples of features of the Human Computer Interface which can be altered by the user.*

Human Computer Interface

15. A good Human Computer Interface is said to be user-friendly.
Explain what this means.

16. Some programs are menu-driven and others are command-driven.

   a) Which type of program is said to be more user-friendly?

   b) Which type of program is usually preferred by more experienced users?

   c) Describe how the user might select what to do next when using a command-driven program.

   d) Describe how the user might select what to do next when using a menu-driven program.

17. Many modern computers use a WIMP system for the user to communicate with the computer.

   a) Explain the meaning of the term WIMP.

   b) Give an alternative name for a WIMP interface.

   c) Explain what the keyboard is used for in a WIMP system.

18. a) What is an icon?

   b) Give **two** examples of icons.

   c) Describe how a user might select an icon in a WIMP system.

19. Briefly describe the difference between an on-line tutorial and on-line help.

See pages 8 and 9 of 'Standard Grade Revision Notes'

Word-processing

20. A word-processor allows the user to <u>enter</u>, <u>amend</u>, <u>delete</u>, save, <u>retrieve</u> and print out text.

    Briefly describe what is meant by each of the underlined terms.

21. Explain the term <u>wordwrap</u> and state why it is often used by word-processors.

22. a) Explain the term <u>tabulation</u>.

    b) What are the typical preset TAB settings in a word-processing system?

    c) Describe what the cursor might look like when using a word-processor.

23. a) A name and address on a letter might be <u>right justified</u>.
    Explain why you might want to right justify the name and address and draw
    a diagram to show what the text would look like.

    b) The text in a book might be <u>left justified</u>.
    Explain why you might want to left justify the text and draw a diagram
    to show what the text would look like.

    c) The columns in a newspaper might be <u>fully justified</u>.
    Explain why you might want to fully justify the columns and draw a diagram
    to show what the text would look like.

24. A spellcheck system allows the spelling of all the words in a word-processed
    document to be checked.

    a) Where are all the words "known" by the system usually kept?

    b) How many words does a typical system "know"?

    c) What sort of words would the system probably NOT "know"?

    d) How does the system "learn" new words?

See page 10 of 'Standard Grade Revision Notes'

25. a) What is a <u>standard paragraph</u>?

    b) Give an example of a situation where standard paragraphs could be used.

26. *a)* *What is a <u>standard letter</u>?*

    b) *The letter, produced on a word-processor, can be linked to another type of file. Name the type of file.*

    c) *What name is given to the process of producing standard letters by combining the word-processed information with that stored on the other type of file?*

Spreadsheets

27. Briefly describe the appearance of a typical spreadsheet.

28. Name the **three** different types of information that a spreadsheet can contain. Give an example to illustrate each type of information.

29. Name **two** types of chart that can be drawn using the data in a spreadsheet and draw a diagram to show the appearance of each one.

30. a) Explain the difference between <u>automatic calculation</u> and <u>manual calculation</u> when referring to the use of a formula in a spreadsheet.

    b) Describe one situation where it would be preferable to use <u>manual calculation</u> and explain why it is preferable.

    c) Which option is usually the 'default'?

31. A spreadsheet is set up to contain the formula shown here in cell C1.

Explain what is meant by the term <u>replication</u> and use the spreadsheet to show the effect of replication of the formula shown in cell C1 down column C.

	A	B	C
1			=A1+B1
2			
3			
4			
5			
6			
7			
8			

32. a) Explain what is meant by the term <u>cell attributes</u> and describe the effect that altering the attributes would have on a number stored in a spreadsheet cell.

b) Describe the effect that changing attributes could have on the date for the first day of January in the year 2000 stored in a spreadsheet cell.

33. *The following formula is stored in a spreadsheet cell:* $B1=IF(A1>31;0;1)$

Explain the meaning of this formula.

34. *When the contents of a cell are replicated the process could be <u>absolute</u> or <u>relative</u>.*

a) *Give examples to illustrate the terms <u>relative replication</u> and <u>absolute replication</u>.*

b) *Name one way in which the spreadsheet can be instructed to make a reference to a cell <u>absolute</u>.*

c) *Describe one situation where the user might want to make a reference to a cell <u>absolute</u>.*

35. *<u>Cell protection</u> is sometimes used to lock parts of a spreadsheet.*

a) *What kinds of information should be locked on a spreadsheet?*

b) *Why might it be desirable to lock these cells?*

See pages 13 and 14 of 'Standard Grade Revision Notes'

Databases

36. A database stored on disc contains the names of ten friends, with their dates of birth and favourite colour.

    Give an example from this to explain each of the terms <u>file</u>, <u>record</u> and <u>field</u>.

37. One operation that can be carried out on a database is <u>searching</u>. The search can be <u>simple</u> or it can be <u>complex</u>.

    Explain what happens when a file is <u>searched</u> and describe the difference between a <u>simple search</u> and a <u>complex search</u>.

38. The information in a database can be displayed in different ways.

    a) Give a name which describes one particular way in which a file is displayed.

    b) Name two ways in which database information is commonly displayed.

39. *a) A field in a database can be <u>computed</u>. Explain what this means.*

    b) What is the advantage to the user in being able to change the input format for data?

    c) What may happen when the format of output from a database is changed?

40. *a) Explain what happens when a database is sorted according to the contents of one field.*

    b) Give an example to show the advantage of sorting a database on <u>two</u> fields.

Graphics

41. a) Describe **three** tools which you may expect to find in a graphics program.

    b) What are tool <u>attributes</u>?

    c) Give **two** examples of the effect of changing tool attributes.

    d) What happens when a graphic is <u>scaled</u>?

Communications

42. a) A computer can be connected to a <u>network</u>. What is a network and what advantages does it have over computers that are not networked?

b) Name the two main types of network and compare them on the basis of the distances involved, the cable system used and the number of transmission errors that occur.

43. A facsimile machine digitises the information on a page and transmits it to another facsimile machine.

a) Give another name for a facsimile machine.

b) Explain what happens when the information is digitised.

44. a) What is needed for someone to be able to use <u>electronic mail</u>?

b) What is an <u>electronic mailbox</u>?

c) Give **one** advantage and **one** disadvantage of electronic mail.

45. a) Teletext is a <u>one-way</u> system. Explain what this means.

b) Name **three** types of information that can be obtained from a teletext service.

c) Give an example of an <u>interactive service</u> on a viewdata system.

d) What is the purpose of a <u>gateway</u> in a viewdata system?

46. a) A device is <u>on-line</u> to the computer. What does this mean?

b) Explain why documents which are to be transmitted electronically are often prepared <u>off-line</u>.

47. a) *Briefly describe the main points of a <u>multi-access system</u>.*

b) *Explain what is meant by the term <u>remote terminal</u>.*

c) *Describe the process of time-slicing and state what effect this has on each user of a multi-access system.*

See pages 18, 19 and 20 of 'Standard Grade Revision Notes'

Integration

48. a) Give **two** examples of operations that can be carried out by multi-task packages.

    b) Give **two** reasons why an integrated package is often easier to use than separate general purpose packages.

49. A chart is drawn from some data contained in a spreadsheet.

The chart can either be <u>dynamically</u> or <u>statically</u> linked to the spreadsheet data. Explain the difference between the two links.

Implications

50. a) Briefly describe **two** effects on jobs that have been brought about by the introduction of computers.

    b) What is a <u>mail shot</u>?

51. a) Briefly describe **three** ways in which a company can protect the data it has stored on computer.

    b) What is a <u>computer hacker</u>?

52. The costs to a business of using computers include both <u>setting up costs</u> and <u>running costs</u>.

    a) Give **two** examples of <u>setting up costs</u>.

    b) Give **two** examples of <u>running costs</u>.

*53. a) State **three** of the main points in the Data Protection Act (1984).*

    b) What is a <u>data user</u>?

See pages 21, 22 and 23 of 'Standard Grade Revision Notes'

Industrial and Commercial Applications
Automated Systems

54. a) Briefly describe **four** benefits to companies which use automated systems.

    b) Explain why an interface is used with automated systems.

55. Two types of signal are used when devices are connected to computer systems: analogue and digital.

    Draw diagrams to show these signals and explain the difference between them.

56. a) What is a sensor and what type of device is it?

    b) Name **three** types of sensor.

57. Name **three** types of output device used with automated systems.

58. a) What is feedback?

    b) What kind of device is attached to output devices to allow feedback to take place?

59. Explain the difference between open loop control and closed loop control.

60. *Explain what is meant when automated computer systems are said to be adaptable.*

61. *A to D and D to A converters are special types of interface. Explain what they are and which is used for input and which for output.*

See pages 24, 25 and 26 of 'Standard Grade Revision Notes'

62. a)   Give a brief explanation of what a <u>robot</u> is.

    b)   Give **three** reasons why a robot is usually not shaped like a human.

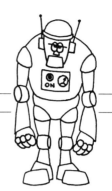

63. Draw a diagram of a robot arm to show the following joints:

    shoulder; elbow; gripper; waist; wrist.

64. a)   What name is used to describe a robot that is fixed in position?

    b)   What do <u>mobile</u> robots usually use to move about?

65. a)   A magnetic guide can be used to guide a mobile robot around a factory. Briefly describe how this system works.

    b)   Name **one** other guidance system for mobile robots.

66. Expand and briefly describe the abbreviations **CNC** and **CAD/CAM**.

67. *a)*   *Explain the term <u>end effector</u>.*

    b)   *Give **two** examples of typical end effectors.*

68. *a)*   *Explain what is meant by the expression 'a robot arm has four degrees of freedom'.*

    b)   *Draw a diagram to show a robot arm with **four** degrees of freedom.*

69. *Explain the terms <u>yaw</u>, <u>pitch</u> and <u>roll</u> as used to describe the movement of a gripper on a robot arm, drawing diagrams of each.*

See pages 26, 27 and 28 of 'Standard Grade Revision Notes'

70. Briefly describe **two** methods of programming robots.

71. a) Which of the following types of language is best for a programmer to use to program a computer that is controlling a robot:

   high level, assembly, low level or machine code?

   b) Explain why you have made this choice.

72. a) Give **three** examples of situations which are suitable for computer simulation. In each case give **one** reason why this is suitable.

   b) Describe how movement and visual effects are typically produced by simulators.

73. a) What is meant when a process is said to take place in <u>real-time</u>?

   b) Give an example of a real-time process.

74. a) Give **one** example of worries employees might have when automated systems are introduced into a factory.

   b) Give **two** examples of benefits to employees from the introduction of automated systems.

   c) Explain why the running costs of factories using automated systems are much lower than those which are not automated.

75. a) *Explain why <u>special control languages</u> were developed for programming automated systems.*

   b) *Other than in backing store, where might the specialised programs be stored?*

Commercial Data Processing

76. a) Briefly describe **three** reasons why companies use computers to process their data.

    b) List the main stages in the data processing cycle.

77. a) Explain the difference between data and information.

    b) Give an example to support your answer.

78. a) Name **three** methods of collection and input of data to a computer which are designed to eliminate operator errors.

    b) Suggest **one** use for each method you have selected.

    c) Explain the difference between direct data entry and key to disc methods of entry.

79. a) What is a check digit?

    b) Give **two** examples of situations where check digits are used.

    c) What characters are usually used as check digits?

    d) Name **two** other types of check that are often made on the data which has been entered into a computer.

80. a) Describe the process of Optical Character Recognition.

    b) What textual features are important when using optical character readers?

    c) Name **two** uses of Optical Character Recognition.

81. What is meant by remote data entry?

    Suggest what extra hardware is required for a computer system to use remote data entry.

See pages 31, 32 and 33 of 'Standard Grade Revision Notes'

82. What is a turnaround document?

Give **two** examples of turnaround documents.

83. Commercial data is typically processed in one of two ways – batch processing and interactive processing.

   a)   Briefly describe each method of processing.

   b)   For each method, give **one** example of a situation where it is used.

84. a)   Give **three** examples of different underlined master files.

   b)   What does a transaction file contain?

   c)   What happens during the process of updating master files?

85. *a)   Explain the term underlined validation of data.*

   b)   Describe the process of underlined double entry of data.

   c)   Of what process is double entry an example?

86. *a)   What type of media is typically used for storing data by underlined sequential access?*

   b)   What type of media is typically used for storing data by underlined direct access?

   c)   Give an alternative name for each of the above storage methods.

   d)   Name a typical use of sequential access files.

87. *a)   In the grandfather-father-son method of file storage, explain what is done if the underlined father master files become corrupted.*

   b)   Which set of files are discarded each day?

See pages 34 and 35 of 'Standard Grade Revision Notes'

88. a) Briefly describe the main hardware required by a large company which processes its data by computer.

b) Output can be to screen, printer or <u>microfiche</u>.

What is microfiche? Give one advantage and one disadvantage of using microfiche.

89. a) Briefly describe the work done by each of the following employees:

programmer; engineer; data preparation operator

b) Name one other job associated with commercial data processing.

90. a) Name some of the <u>initial costs</u> involved when a company decides to use commercial data processing.

b) Name some of the <u>running costs</u> involved when a company uses commercial data processing.

91. a) What is a <u>point-of-sale terminal</u>?

b) What advantage to the company exists when point-of-sale terminals are used?

c) Explain the process of <u>electronic funds transfer</u>.

92. a) *Commercial data processed output can be to file. What happens to the file at a later stage?*

b) *Name **two** different types of file that may be used.*

93. *Briefly describe **two** examples of computer crime.*

94. Security is very important to commercial organisations. One method of keeping files secure is to allow access by the use of passwords.

    a)   Describe what happens on such a system when a user wants to access the information.

    b)   Why might there be more than one password in use?

    c)   Describe **one** other method of maintaining security of data.

95. Some commercial companies will sell lists of their customers to other companies.

What advantage is there for the company buying the lists?

96. Briefly compare the manual system by which companies maintain their records with a modern computerised system.

3. Computer Systems

Systems software

97. a)   Describe the main features of high level languages.

    b)   What name is given to the process of turning a high level language program into machine code?

98. *a)   What is a <u>general purpose language</u>?*

    Give an example of a general purpose language.

    b)   What is a <u>special purpose language</u>?

    Give an example of a special purpose language.

See pages 38 and 39 of 'Standard Grade Revision Notes'

99. a) Explain the difference between <u>source code</u> and <u>object code</u> when using a compiler.

b) Explain what a programmer must do when making changes to a compiled program.

c) Explain why interpreted programs run more slowly than compiled programs.

Operating and Filing Systems

100. a) What is an operating system?

b) Name **four** of the functions of an operating system.

c) What advantage is there in storing the operating system in RAM rather than ROM?

101. a) What is the difference between <u>data files</u> and <u>program files</u>?

b) Give an example of each type of file.

c) What is the purpose of a directory on a disc?

102. Some of the specialised functions of an operating system are <u>multiprogramming</u>, <u>multi-access</u> and <u>resource allocation</u>.

a) Briefly describe each of these functions.

b) Give an alternative name for <u>multi-access</u>.

103. Interactive operating systems can often carry out <u>background tasks</u>.

a) Why are these tasks suited to interactive systems?

b) Give **one** example of a <u>background task</u>.

Low Level Machine

104. Explain the terms <u>bit</u>, <u>byte</u>, <u>kilobyte</u>, <u>megabyte</u> and <u>gigabyte</u>.

105. a) Draw a diagram to show the relationship between <u>input</u>, <u>output</u>, <u>process</u> and <u>backing store</u>. Add arrows to show the direction in which data flows.

    b) Name the **two** main parts of the <u>Central Processing Unit</u>.

106. a) Explain why the execution of machine code is much faster than the execution of a high level language.

    b) Give **two** reasons why programmers do not program in machine code.

107. a) Explain why the binary number 1110 represents the decimal number 14.

    b) Give the decimal place values for each of the eight digits in an 8 bit number.

108. Textual information in a computer is represented by ASCII codes for each character.

    a) Expand the term <u>ASCII</u>.

    b) Give an example of an ASCII code and the character it represents.

    c) How many bytes are needed to store each character represented by an ASCII code?

109. a) Explain the term <u>word</u> when used in computing.

    b) What is meant by the term <u>addressability</u>?

    c) Give an example of a typical addressability of a modern computer system.

110. a) What is a <u>pixel</u>?

b) Explain how the <u>resolution</u> of graphics depends on the number of pixels used.

111. a) What is a <u>character set</u>?

b) What differences might there be between different character sets?

112. *Give **two** examples to describe the function of <u>control characters</u>.*

113. *a) Explain the term <u>integer number</u>.*

b) What is the range of integer <u>binary</u> numbers if eight bits are available to store them?

c) What is this range as decimal values?

114. *Computers store numbers which may not be whole numbers as a <u>mantissa</u> and <u>exponent</u>.*

a) Give a name for this storage method.

b) Give an example of a <u>binary</u> number stored as a mantissa and exponent. Indicate which part is the mantissa and which the exponent.

115. *a) What is the purpose of the <u>control unit</u> in the Central Processing Unit?*

b) Name a typical logic operation carried out in the Arithmetic and Logic Unit.

Hardware

116. a)   Give **two** differences between <u>ROM</u> and <u>RAM</u>.

    b)   Name **two** different types of magnetic media.

    c)   Describe **two** precautions to be taken when using magnetic media.

117. a)   Name **four** different <u>input</u> devices.

    b)   Name **four** different <u>output</u> devices.

118. Name **one** backing storage device that does not use magnetic media and give the typical storage capacity of the media it uses.

119. a)   Name **one** specialised <u>input</u> device and suggest who might use it.

    b)   Name **one** specialised <u>output</u> device.

120. An advertisement for a new computer system describes it as a <u>multimedia</u> system.

Describe the typical hardware which you would expect such a system to have and why it is needed.

Printed by Inglis Allen, Kirkcaldy

Answers to

QUESTIONS
in STANDARD GRADE
COMPUTING STUDIES

Arlen Pardoe

and

Kevin Thompson

This section of the book gives specimen answers to the questions.

However, it is only your teacher who can tell you if

your answer is good enough.

Published by
Leckie & Leckie
8 Whitehill Terrace
St. Andrews
Scotland KY16 8RN
Tel. 01334 475656
Fax. 01334 477392
email: s.leckie@leckie-and-leckie.co.uk
web: www.leckie-and-leckie.co.uk

Edited by
Neil Kennedy

Thanks also to
Bruce Ryan, Hamish Sanderson and Fiona McNee

ISBN 1-898890-45-5

A CIP Catalogue record is available from the British Library.

Printed in Scotland by Inglis Allen on environmentally-friendly paper. The paper is made from a mixture of sawmill waste, forest thinnings and wood from sustainable forests.

Leckie & Leckie

2. Computer Applications

General Purpose Packages

System Requirements

1. a) Processor speed typically over 25 MHz on older computers and over 200 MHz on newer computers.

   b) One or more floppy drives and a hard disc drive. Other backing storage devices (such as Zip, Jaz and optical drives) are also common.

   c) QWERTY keyboard, mouse, high resolution monitor, high quality printer (inkjet or laser).

2. a) A desktop computer is fairly large, mains-powered and fits on a desk.

   b) A laptop computer is smaller than a desktop computer. It is light and portable and is powered by battery or mains.

   c) A palmtop computer is smaller than a laptop computer. It is small enough to hold in one hand. It has small keys and is battery-powered.

3. a) To store data and to make backup copies.

   b) They can print text and graphics, are high quality and are quiet in operation.

4. a) *An Expert System is a computerised databank which can imitate some of the functions of a human expert in a small area of expertise. It answers questions using facts and rules entered into the knowledge base.*

   b) *Giving legal advice (lawyers); helping medical diagnosis (doctors).*

Storage

5. • Numeric data – for example: 2.34

   • Textual data – for example: 43 High Street

   • Graphic data – for example:

   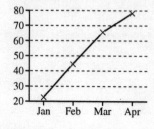

Answers page 2

6. a) The process of regularly making copies is called backup.

    b) It is important to make backup copies because the original file could be lost or damaged. This could happen accidentally or it might be deliberate.

7. a) *A 5.25" floppy disc typically stores between 100 Kb and 1.4 Mb.*

    b) *A 3.5" floppy disc typically stores between 800 Kb and 1.4 Mb.*

    c) *A fixed hard disc typically stores between 20 Mb and 540 Mb on older computers and in excess of 1.0 Gb on newer computers.*

    d) *A CD-ROM typically stores 700 Mb.*

Need for GPPs

8. Three tasks which people wanted a computer to do in the 1980s were:

    - typing in and editing data

    - doing calculations with data

    - presenting information as graphs and pictures.

9. a) *A database stores information in an organised way, which makes it easy to retrieve.*

    b) *A word-processor stores text and can bring together information from other general purpose packages.*

    c) *A spreadsheet processes figures and produces accounts. It can also display charts and graphs using the spreadsheet information.*

    To send the information electronically from office to office requires extra hardware (a modem and access to telephone lines) and software (communications software).

Common Features

10. a) The process <u>Open</u> will load a document which has been saved on backing store.

    b) The process <u>Print part</u> prints only a part of the document, such as a single page or a selected area.

    c) The process <u>Amend data</u> alters some data in the document, such as making the line length larger or changing the spelling of a word.

    d) The process <u>Copy data</u> copies the data that has been marked in some way. It is then ready to be pasted somewhere else.

    e) The process <u>Move data</u> takes the data that has been selected and moves it to another place in the document.

11. The font can be changed. This gives the characters a different shape.

    The character size can be changed to make the text smaller or larger.

    The style of the text can be changed to make it bold or underlined.

12. *A printer driver is software which is selected by the user. This allows different printers to work properly with a particular computer by selecting the appropriate printer driver.*

13. *A header is placed at the top of every page in the document and may contain text or graphics. The information will be mainly the same on each page, although automatic page numbering can be set to give a different page number on each page. A footer is similar to a header except it appears at the bottom of a page.*

14. a) *The Human Computer Interface controls how the computer system appears to the user as the user interacts with it to change data and control programs.*

    b) *Examples of features of the Human Computer Interface that the user can alter are the size of a window and the colour in which text is displayed.*

Human Computer Interface

15. A user-friendly Human Computer Interface is one which is easy to use. This means that the user can easily understand what to do and what is happening with the computer system.

16. a) Menu-driven is more user-friendly.

    b) Command-driven is usually preferred by experienced users.

    c) In a command-driven program the user selects what to do next by typing in a command in a special language.

    d) In a menu-driven program the user selects what to do by making a selection from a menu printed on the screen by the computer. This may involve typing a letter or number or using a mouse to indicate the required option.

17. a) WIMP stands for Windows, Icons, Mouse and Pull-down menu (alternatively Windows, Icons, Menus and Pointers).

    b) An alternative name for a WIMP interface is a Graphical User Interface (or GUI).

    c) In a WIMP system the keyboard is used to enter text and numbers.

18. a) An icon is a small picture on the screen used to represent items which can be selected or used.

    b) Two examples of icons are the wastebasket and a floppy disc:

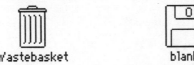

    c) The user could select an icon by moving the mouse until the pointer is pointing at the icon, then pressing the mouse button to highlight the icon.

19. An on-line tutorial takes you stage by stage through the different features of the program.

    On-line help can be accessed while the program is running. It is usually arranged in help menus, which allow the user to choose the part of the program for which help is needed.

Word-processing

20. The term <u>enter</u> means to type in text.

    The term <u>amend</u> means to alter text already present.

    The term <u>delete</u> means to remove text.

    The term <u>retrieve</u> means to load back into the computer the text that has been saved on backing store.

21. Wordwrap is the process that occurs when a word is typed in towards the end of a line. If the word is too long to fit into the space available, the whole word is moved to the start of the next line.

    It is often used by word-processors to avoid words being split between two lines.

22. a) Tabulation uses preset positions along a line. The cursor is moved to these positions by pressing the TAB key.

    b) Typical TAB settings are every half inch.

    c) The cursor often looks like a flashing line in the text.

23. a) So that the name and address appear on the right-hand side of the page.

    b) Normal text in a book is usually set up to be left justified with the text lined up on the left-hand side of the page.

    c) Newspaper columns are usually fully justified so that both left- and right-hand sides are lined up.

24. a) The words known by the system are usually kept in a separate file called a dictionary.

   b) A typical system knows about 50 000 words.

   c) The system would probably not know names of people or towns.

   d) The system can learn new words by adding them to its dictionary file.

25. a) A standard paragraph is used many times to make different letters.

   b) Standard paragraphs can be used when the same text is used in many different documents, such as a company giving details on a delayed order.

26. *a) A standard letter is one which is sent to many people with only a few details changed, such as names and addresses.*

   b) A standard letter file may be linked to a database file.

   c) The process is mail merge.

Spreadsheets

27. A typical spreadsheet is a table or grid made up of cells which are named from the column and rows which they occupy.

28. The three types of information that a spreadsheet can contain are numbers, text and formulas. For example: 23, total, =A2+B3

29. Two types of chart that could be drawn using data in a spreadsheet are bar charts and pie charts.

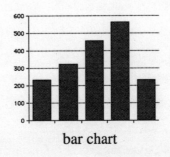

bar chart

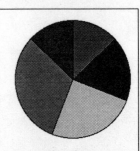

pie chart

30. a) Automatic calculation causes the spreadsheet to recalculate all the values in formulas every time a new value or formula is entered. With manual calculation the recalculation is only done when an instruction is given to the spreadsheet to do it.

b) It would be preferable to use manual calculation if large numbers of formulas or values are to be entered or changed. This would allow quicker entry of the new data without time being taken to calculate after each one was entered.

c) The default option is usually automatic calculation.

---

31. Replication is the process where the contents of one cell are copied to other cells, adjusting for the column and row references in any formulas used.

In the example, the cells below C1 would contain the formula
=A2+B2 in cell C2,
=A3+B3 in cell C3 .... and so on.

C
=A1+B1
=A2+B2
=A3+B3
=A4+B4

---

32. a) Cell attributes refers to the options for the display of data in cells in different ways.
For example, the number 2.987 could be displayed as 2.987, 3, 2.99 or £2.98 depending on the attributes chosen.

b) The date could be displayed as 1/1/00 or January 1, 2000.

---

33. *This causes the cell B1 to have the value 0 if the contents of cell A1 are greater than 31. If this is not so (A1 contents are 31 or less) then B1 will contain the value 1.*

---

34. a) *Relative replication of cells causes the column and row references in formulas to change according to the row and column into which the cell is copied.*
For example, if cell C1 contains the formula =A1*B1
and this is copied relatively into cell C2, the new formula would be =A1*B2.

	A	B	C
1			=A1*B1
2			=A2*B2

The same process carried out using absolute replication would result in cell C2 containing the same formula as that in cell C1, that is =A1*B1.

	A	B	C
1			=A1*B1
2			=A1*B1

b) *A dollar sign is often placed in front of the row or column reference to make it absolute, for example A1*B1.*

c) *A user may wish to make a cell reference absolute when a fixed cell is always to be referred to in a formula, for example the rate of VAT for all VAT calculations.*

35. *a)* *Information should be locked in cells where the data is not to be changed by the user, for example text for headings or fixed values and formulas.*

b) *It is desirable to lock these cells so that the user cannot accidentally change their contents.*

Databases

36. A <u>file</u> is the complete set of data stored on disc. A <u>record</u> is the data for one person – their name, date of birth and favourite colour. A <u>field</u> is one of the separate pieces of information for one person – their date of birth, for example.

37. A file is searched to find those records which match what is being looked for.

A simple search checks for the contents of only one field. A complex search uses at least two fields.

38. a) The way in which a particular file is displayed is called the format or layout.

b) Common formats are card format and list format.

39. *a)* *A computed field is one where the contents have been calculated using a formula, usually using the contents of other fields in the calculation.*

b) *By changing the input format, data entry can be made simpler, for example by matching the data entry to that on a form containing the data.*

c) *The output format can display the output in different ways, not necessarily showing all the fields. So, the fields may be shown in a different order and position.*

40. *a)* *The order of all the records is changed, placing them in the order determined by the way in which they are sorted on the selected field.*

b) *This allows two sorts to be done in one operation. For example, sorting a list of names into alphabetical order of surname **and** forename.*

Graphics

41. a) Three examples of tools in a graphics program are line, circle and rectangle drawing tools.

    b) Tool attributes are the properties of the object, i.e. how the object appears.

    c) Two examples are changing the thickness of a line and the fill pattern of a circle.

    d) When a graphic is scaled, it is made larger or smaller.

Communications

42. a) A network is a set of computers and peripherals joined together by cables. This allows expensive peripherals to be used by more than one computer. This keeps costs down, while making the peripherals available to all the computers. It also allows files to be shared.

    b) Local Area Networks (LANs) and Wide Area Networks (WANs).

    LANs operate over fairly small distances, typically a room or building, use simple and inexpensive cabling and have few transmission errors.

    WANs operate over large distances, e.g. between towns or countries, use more expensive cabling and commonly have more frequent transmission errors.

43. a) A facsimile machine is often simply called a fax.

    b) When the information is digitised, it is turned into binary numbers which can be sent through the telephone system.

44. a) Electronic mail requires a computer system, communications software, a modem and access to telephone lines. A subscription to an e-mail service is also required.

    b) An electronic mailbox is an area of a computer's memory where messages can be left for other users to read by making a connection to the system.

    c) One advantage is that a message can be sent to many people in one operation. A disadvantage is that the correct equipment is required.

45. a) The teletext one-way system only allows the information to be sent in one direction – from the central computer to that of the user.

b) Three types of teletext information are news, sport and weather information.

c) An example of a viewdata interactive service is booking plane tickets. The user can check on seat availability and send a booking back to the central computer.

d) A gateway allows two different computer networks to be connected together.

46. a) On-line means a device is connected to, and communicating with, the computer.

b) Because phone connection time costs money, it is more economical to prepare documents off-line, therefore not using phone time to type in the information.

47. a) *In a multi-access system many users have a terminal which is connected to a mainframe computer. The terminal is a keyboard and screen which is using the processing power of the mainframe computer.*

b) *A remote terminal is located some distance from the mainframe computer and uses modems to connect to the mainframe.*

c) *Time slicing occurs when each user is allocated a short period of time in turn to be connected to the mainframe. Because the mainframe computer operates very quickly, each user appears to have sole use of the mainframe.*

Integration

48. a) Typical multi-task operations are the creation of charts from spreadsheet data and the ability to draw simple shapes in a word-processor.

b) Pull-down menus in all parts of the integrated package are similar and key combinations for common tasks such as printing a document are the same.

49. *If the link is static then it exists only as long as the data is being transferred from the spreadsheet to the chart. Once this has taken place, the link is broken. Further changes to the spreadsheet data will not appear as changes to the chart.*

If the link is dynamic then it is not broken after transfer and further changes to the spreadsheet data will cause the chart to show the new values.

Implications

50. a) Page layout by compositors is now done electronically using desktop publishing software. Typists have now become word-processor operators.

    b) Large numbers of names and addresses are taken from a database and used for labels on envelopes to send material to many people.

51. a) Companies can protect data stored on computer by keeping computer room doors locked, by requiring a password to gain access to important files and by keeping backup copies of vital information in fireproof safes.

    b) A computer hacker is someone who tries to gain access to a computer system when they do not have permission for access.

52. a) Setting up costs for businesses include the cost of the hardware (e.g. computer systems and printers) and software costs (e.g. programs and application packages).

    b) Running costs for business computers include equipment repairs and cost of consumables (e.g. paper, toner and discs).

53. a) *The Data Protection Act (1984) requires companies to register if they wish to hold data about more than a few people. It only allows data to be stored for lawful purposes. People have the right to check the accuracy of data stored about them (with some exceptions, such as police files).*

    b) *A data user is someone who has, or controls, personal data about other people.*

Industrial and Commercial Applications

Automated Systems

54. a) Benefits to companies which use automated systems include:
tasks can be carried out more quickly; high accuracy of manufacture; tasks can be done in hot or cold conditions where humans cannot work; greater efficiency, as more goods can be produced for less cost.

    b) An interface is used to allow for differences in the speed of different devices, and for differences in the devices' codes for handling data.

55. a) An analogue signal has a wide range of values which are constantly changing.

    Analogue signal – many levels

    A digital signal can only be one of two values (0 or 1).

    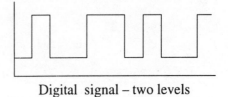

    Digital signal – two levels

56. a) A sensor detects events such as heat and light level changing. It is an INPUT device.

    b) Three sensors are a heat sensor, a light sensor and a movement sensor.

57. Three output devices used with automated systems are a heater, a motor and a lamp.

58. a) Feedback occurs when information is returned to the CPU from a device controlled by a computer.

    b) Feedback is provided by sensors placed on the output device.

59. Open loop control takes place when there is no feedback from the device controlled by the computer. The computer cannot tell if an instruction has been carried out.

    Closed loop control occurs when feedback between the device and computer occurs. The computer program does know if the required action has taken place.

60. *Automated systems which are adaptable can be easily reprogrammed to do different tasks.*

61. *An A to D convertor converts analogue signals to digital signals. It is used for input.*
    A D to A convertor converts digital information to analogue. It is an output device.

62. a) A robot is a machine, controlled by a computer, which is flexible – that means it can be made to do more than one task by reprogramming it.

    b) A robot is not shaped like a human because the robot might overbalance as the body is top heavy; it is difficult to make robots walk like humans and the size and shape might be unsuitable for the task to be done.

63.

64. a) A robot in a fixed position is a stationary robot.

    b) Mobile robots usually use wheels or tracks to move about.

65. a) A wire is buried in the ground. When an electric current is passed through the wire, a magnetic field is generated. Sensors on the mobile robot sense this and so can follow the wire.

    b) A white-line follower.

66. CNC stands for Computer Numerical Control. Numbers are sent to the machine to control its movement. Sensors detect if the operation has been carried out.

CAD/CAM stands for Computer Aided Design/Computer Aided Manufacture. The computer is used both in the design process and manufacture, with details of the design being passed on to the manufacturing process.

67. a) *An end effector is a tool which can be used by a robot arm. It is able to be exchanged for other end effectors to allow different jobs to be done.*

b) *Examples of typical end effectors are grippers and ladles.*

68. a) *Degrees of freedom refers to the number of different ways in which a robot arm can move. Four degrees of freedom means the robot has four joints at which movement takes place.*

b)

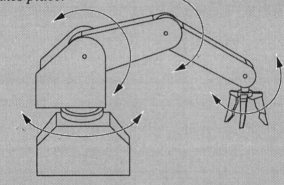

69. *Yaw is a side-to-side movement, pitch is an up-and-down movement and roll is a rotational movement of the gripper:*

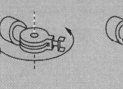 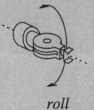

          yaw   *pitch*   *roll*

70. Robots can be programmed using a program which tells them exactly what to do. Robots can also be programmed by the 'lead-through' method where a human operator, connected to sensors, shows the computer what to do.

71. a) A high level language is often best for the programmer to use.

b) It is easy for the programmer to make changes and correct any errors in the program.

72. a) Computer simulation is suitable: for practising defusing bombs which is dangerous; for learning to fly aeroplanes which is expensive and for learning to control nuclear power stations which is also dangerous.

b) Movement in simulators may be made by hydraulic systems and visual effects can be provided on large screens.

73. a) Real-time processes use the computer to process events as they occur. What the computer does next depends on what has just happened.

b) An example of a real-time process is in an automated factory. There must be an immediate response if a breakdown occurs.

74. a) Employees might worry that they will not be able to understand the new machines and so lose their jobs, or that they will find it difficult to learn new skills.

b) Employees will have better working conditions and more leisure time.

c) Running costs in automated factories are lower because fewer workers are required; areas where only machines work do not need the same levels of light or heat that humans require; the only costs are the repair and maintenance of equipment.

75. a) *Special control languages were developed for automated systems because some of the instructions the operator needs to use are specific to the needs of the machines.*

b) *The specialised programs might be stored in customised ROM.*

Commercial Data Processing

76. a) Companies use computers for data processing because there is a very large amount to be processed daily, computers are very fast at the processing and they process the data accurately.

b) The main stages in the data processing cycle are data collection, data preparation, data input, data processing, storage of data and output of data.

77. a) Data is any information that can be stored in a computer and can be meaningless without further explanation. Information is data in a form that humans can understand.

b) An example of data is a simple number like 12345. This could mean almost anything.
When it is put into context it is meaningful, such as cost of new car = £12345.

78. a) Bar codes, kimball tags and magnetic stripes are three methods of data collection designed to eliminate operator errors.

b) Bar codes are used on books, kimball tags on clothing and magnetic stripes on cheque cards.

c) Direct data entry is the entry of data at the keyboard which is immediately passed to the computer and processed. Key to disc input takes the data entered at the keyboard and stores it on disc. At some later stage the data on disc is passed to the computer for processing.

79. a) A check digit is an extra digit added to numerical data to check that the data has been entered correctly into the computer. The original digit is calculated from the other numbers. The computer then recalculates the check digit and compares the result with the value entered.

b) Check digits are used in ISBN numbers and credit card numbers.

c) The characters used for check digits are usually the numbers 0 to 9 and the letter X.

d) Two other checks on the data entered are range checks and length checks.

80. a) *Optical Character Recognition reads characters on paper and inputs the data into a computer.*

b) *The font and size of characters are important.*

c) *Reading documents to save having to retype them into the computer; reading the line of reference numbers printed on some electricity bills.*

81. *Remote data entry happens when the computer processing the data is separate from the place where data entry takes place. It may be on a totally different site.*

A modem is used at each end to connect the sites together through telephone lines.

82. A turnaround document is one which is printed out by computer, is filled in and then returned for the data to be entered into a computer.

Electricity bills and mail order forms are turnaround documents.

83. a) Batch processing collects the data to be processed over a period of time and feeds the collected data, together with the program, into the computer. The program is started and continues to run until the whole batch of data has been processed.

Interactive processing has a program running all the time and processes data immediately. The result of this processing affects the next action of the computer.

b) Batch processing is used for processing payrolls; interactive processing is used for operating bank accounts.

84. a) Customer, stock and payroll files are examples of master files.

b) A transaction file contains details of changes since the last update of master files, such as a day's business.

c) The transaction and master files are merged to produce updated master files.

85. *a)* *Validation of data checks to see if the data is within prescribed limits, such as the days in a month in the range 1 to 31.*

b) *Double entry requires the same data to be entered by two different operators.*

c) *Verification*

86. *a)* *Magnetic tape stores data by sequential access.*

b) *Magnetic disc stores data by direct access.*

c) *Sequential access is also called serial access; direct access is also called random access.*

d) *Sequential access files are typically used for backup purposes.*

87. a) If the father master files are damaged, they can be regenerated using the grandfather master files and the corresponding transaction files.

b) Each day the old grandfather master files and associated transaction files are discarded.

88. a) A mainframe computer would be required; many terminals would be connected, together with several high speed printers, magnetic tape and magnetic disc backing storage devices.

b) Microfiche is a sheet of film material on which a very small copy of the output is printed. One sheet of microfiche can store very many pages but it requires a special magnifying reader to read it.

89. a) A programmer writes programs and modifies existing programs. An engineer maintains and repairs computer systems. A data preparation operator enters data into a computer, usually using a keyboard.

b) One other job is a systems analyst.

90. a) Initial costs include computers, printers, backing storage, software, buildings, furniture and telephone systems.

b) Running costs include salaries, staff training, electricity, consumables, repairs and rentals.

91. a) A point-of-sale terminal is programmed with the prices of all the items in the shop. It can scan each item and automatically give the price.

b) There is little chance of pricing mistakes.

c) Electronic funds transfer does not use notes or coins. Instead, the customer's account at the bank has funds removed and transferred to the business's account by computer.

92. a) At a later stage the file will be processed by the computer.

b) The file may be a print spool file or a partially processed file.

93. Information is stolen to find out about prices so that a lower bid could be made for a job. Deliberate destruction of data could put a competitor out of business.

94. a) The user types in the password when asked. The password does not appear on the screen. If the password is correct then the user gains access to the system.

b) Different passwords and user names give access to different types of data and files (different levels of access).

c) One other method could be to keep the building secure (keeping doors locked), only allowing access to people who work there.

95. The company will buy lists of people who are suited to its purposes, for example people living in a certain part of the country or with particular interests.

96. In the manual system, data is entered on large amounts of paper which have to be stored and kept in order. This requires many staff. In the computerised system, less staff are required with much less paper because the files are on backing storage.

3. Computer Systems

Systems software

97. a) High level languages use English words to give instructions to a computer. One high level language instruction represents several machine code instructions. The instructions are carried out in sequence. Most have commands for process, repetition and decisions. High level languages are designed to solve problems.

b) Translation is the process of turning a high level language program into machine code.

98. a) *A general purpose language is one that can do a variety of computing tasks. An example is PL/1.*

b) *A special purpose language is one developed for a particular type of application. An example is COBOL.*

99. a) *Source code is the text program written on a word-processor. When this is compiled, it produces the object code. It is the object code which is executed when the program is run.*

b) *A programmer must go to the source code, make the changes, then compile the program again to produce new object code.*

c) *A compiled program is already in machine code and ready to be executed. An interpreted program has to be translated as each line is met, and then executed. The translation takes time and so the program runs more slowly.*

Operating and Filing Systems

100. a) An operating system is a set of programs which gives instructions to the computer. It takes control when the computer is first switched on.

b) Four functions are memory management, file management, input/output control and scheduling of jobs.

c) If stored in RAM, the operating system can easily be changed and updated.

101. a) Data files contain the data used by programs. Program files contain the instructions that tell the computer what to do.

b) An example of a data file is the text file produced by a word-processing program. An example of a program file is the word-processing program itself.

c) A directory on a disc contains information about the files on the disc, their names and where they are kept on the disc.

102. a) *Multiprogramming uses several programs in memory at once. The operating system allocates processor time to each in turn.*
Multi-access has several terminals connected to the processor. Each one has a short period of time allocated to it in turn but appears to the user to have sole use of the processor.
Resource allocation is the process carried out by the processor when it connects and disconnects to different resources, as they are required by the program in use.

b) *Multi-access is also known as time-sharing.*

103. a) *Background tasks are suited to interactive systems because there are always times when the processor is otherwise idle, waiting for something to happen. It is at these times the processor can perform background tasks until the main program requires the processor again.*

b) *One example is background printing. Data can be sent to the printer whenever the main application is not using the processor.*

Low Level Machine

104. A <u>bit</u> is a binary digit (a 1 or a 0). A <u>byte</u> is a group of eight bits. A <u>kilobyte</u> is approximately 1000 bytes (exactly 1024 bytes). A <u>megabyte</u> is approximately 1000 kilobytes (exactly 1024 kilobytes). A <u>gigabyte</u> is approximately 1000 megabytes (exactly 1024 megabytes).

105. a)

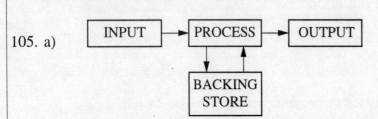

b)   The processor and main memory are the two main parts of the CPU.

106. a)   The machine code does not have to be translated before being executed and so runs faster than a high level language.

b)   Machine code is difficult for humans to understand and errors are difficult to detect and correct.

107. a)   The place values are as shown here:

place value	8	4	2	1
binary number	1	1	1	0

the decimal equivalent is: 1*8 + 1*4 + 1*2 + 0*1 = 14

b)   The place values are: 128, 64, 32, 16, 8, 4, 2, 1.

108. a)   ASCII stands for American Standard Code for Information Interchange.

b)   ASCII code 65 represents the character A.

c)   One byte is required to store each character.

109. *a)   In computing terms, a word is a collection of bits treated as a single unit by the processor. This is usually the number of bits moved as a group, typically 8, 16 or 32 bits.*

b)   Addressability relates to the number of unique addresses that the processor can normally use.

c)   Typical addressabilities of modern computers range from 16 Mb up to 4096 Mb.

110. a)   A pixel is a picture element, the smallest element of a graphic. It can be on or off to turn the colour on or off.

   b)   The greater the number of pixels used to show a graphic of a given size, the higher the resolution.

111. a)   A character set is the group of characters represented by a range of ASCII codes.

   b)   With different character sets, the same ASCII code might represent different characters. For example, in one set a code may be the character D and in another set it might represent the character Δ.

112. *Two examples of the function of control characters include moving the cursor back one space and clearing the screen.*

113. *a)   An integer number is a whole number.*

   b)   The range of binary integer numbers which can be stored in eight bits is from 00000000 to 11111111.

   c)   As decimal numbers the range is from 0 to 255.

114. *a)   When numbers are stored as mantissa and exponent this is called floating point format.*

   b)   An example of a binary number stored in floating point format is:

$$1001011010010110 \times 2^{10010110}$$

   The mantissa is the number 1001011010010110 and the exponent is the number 10010110.

115. *a)   The control unit supervises the decoding and execution of program instructions. Operations inside the processor and flow of data between memory and processor are involved.*

   b)   A typical logic operation in the ALU is an AND operation.

116. a) ROM contents can only be read – they cannot be changed. The contents are permanent – when the computer is switched off, they are not lost.

   RAM contents can be read and altered. The contents are not permanent – when the computer is switched off, they are lost.

   b) Two types of magnetic media are tapes and discs.

   c) Two precautions to be taken with magnetic media are not to touch the media surface and to keep the media away from dirt.

117. a) Four examples of input devices are a keyboard, a mouse, a scanner and a light pen.

   b) Four examples of output devices are a printer, a plotter, a monitor and a loudspeaker.

118. *A backing storage device that is not magnetic is an optical disc drive.*

   Its typical capacity is 128 Mb.

119. *a) An example of a specialised input device is a blowpipe.*
   It might be used by a disabled person.

   b) An example of a specialised output device is a virtual reality helmet.

120. *A multimedia system will use a variety of hardware. This may include CD-ROM players and laser disc players because CD-ROMS and laser discs can store large amounts of data. Suitable output devices will be needed, such as high resolution monitors and high quality sound reproduction systems.*

Kerry Young, Dan Evans & Ron H

ESSENTIALS

AQA GCSE

Further Additional Science

Contents

Contents

How Science Works Overview

How Science Works – Explanation

The AQA GCSE Biology specification incorporates:

- **Science Content** – all the scientific explanations and evidence that you need to know for the exams. (It is covered on pages 12–59 of this revision guide.)
- **How Science Works** – a set of key concepts, relevant to all areas of science. It covers…
  - the relationship between scientific evidence, and scientific explanations and theories
  - how scientific evidence is collected
  - how reliable and valid scientific evidence is
  - the role of science in society
  - the impact science has on our lives
  - how decisions are made about the ways science and technology are used in different situations, and the factors affecting these decisions.

Your teacher(s) will have taught these two types of content together in your science lessons. Likewise, the questions on your exam papers will probably combine elements from both types of content. So, to answer them, you'll need to recall and apply the relevant scientific facts and knowledge of how science works.

The key concepts of How Science Works are summarised in this section of the revision guide (pages 6–11). You should be familiar with all of these concepts. If there is anything you are unsure about, ask your teacher to explain it to you.

How Science Works is designed to help you learn about and understand the practical side of science. It aims to help you develop your skills when it comes to…

- evaluating information
- developing arguments
- drawing conclusions.

The Thinking Behind Science

Science attempts to explain the world we live in.

Scientists carry out investigations and collect evidence in order to…

- **explain phenomena** (i.e. how and why things happen)
- **solve problems** using evidence.

Scientific knowledge and understanding can lead to the **development of new technologies** (e.g. in medicine and industry), which have a huge impact on **society** and the **environment**.

The Purpose of Evidence

Scientific evidence provides **facts** that help to answer a specific question and either **support** or **disprove** an idea or theory. Evidence is often based on data that has been collected through **observations** and **measurements.**

To allow scientists to reach conclusions, evidence must be…

- **repeatable** – other people should be able to repeat the same process
- **reproducible** – other people should be able to reproduce the same results
- **valid** – it must be repeatable, reproducible and answer the question.

N.B. If data isn't repeatable and reproducible, it can't be valid.

To ensure scientific evidence is repeatable, reproducible and valid, scientists look at ideas relating to…

- observations
- investigations
- measurements
- data presentation
- conclusions and evaluation.

How Science Works Overview

Observations

Most scientific investigations begin with an **observation**. A scientist observes an event or phenomenon and decides to find out more about how and why it happens.

The first step is to develop a **hypothesis**, which suggests an explanation for the phenomenon. Hypotheses normally suggest a relationship between two or more **variables** (factors that change).

Hypotheses are based on…
- careful observations
- existing scientific knowledge
- some creative thinking.

The hypothesis is used to make a **prediction**, which can be tested through scientific investigation. The data collected from the investigation will…
- support the hypothesis **or**
- show it to be untrue (refute it) **or**
- lead to the modification of the original hypothesis or the development of a new hypothesis.

If the hypothesis and models we have available to us do not completely match our data or observations, we need to check the validity of our observations or data, or amend the models.

Sometimes, if the new observations and data are valid, existing theories and explanations have to be revised or amended, and so scientific knowledge grows and develops.

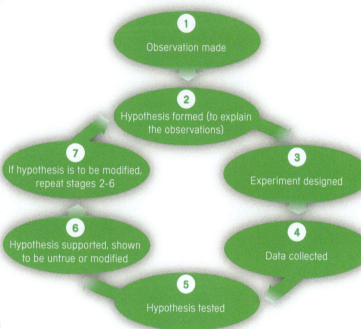

1. Observation made
2. Hypothesis formed (to explain the observations)
3. Experiment designed
4. Data collected
5. Hypothesis tested
6. Hypothesis supported, shown to be untrue or modified
7. If hypothesis is to be modified, repeat stages 2-6

Example
- Two scientists **observe** that freshwater shrimp are only found in certain parts of a stream.
- They use scientific knowledge of shrimp and water flow to develop a **hypothesis**, which relates the presence of shrimp (dependent variable) to the rate of water flow (independent variable). For example, a hypothesis could be: the faster the water flows, the fewer shrimps are found.
- They **predict** that shrimp are only found in parts of the stream where the water flow rate is below a certain value.
- They **investigate** by counting and recording the number of shrimp in different parts of the stream, where water-flow rates differ.
- The **data** shows that more shrimp are present in parts of the stream where the flow rate is below a certain value. So, the data **supports** the hypothesis. But, it also shows that shrimp aren't always present in these parts of the stream.
- The scientists realise there must be another factor affecting the distribution of shrimp. They **refine their hypothesis**.

Investigations

An **investigation** involves collecting data to find out whether there is a relationship between two **variables**. A variable is a factor that can take different values.

In an investigation there are two types of variables:

- **Independent** variable – can be changed by the person carrying out the investigation. For example, the amount of water a plant receives.
- **Dependent** variable – measured each time a change is made to the independent variable, to see if it also changes. For example, the growth rate of the plant (measured by recording the number of leaves).

For a measurement to be valid it must measure only the appropriate variable.

Variables can have different types of values:

- **Continuous variables** – can take any numerical value (including decimals). These are usually measurements, e.g. temperature.
- **Categoric variables** – a variable described by a label, usually a word, e.g. different breeds of dog or blood group.
  - **Discrete variables** – only take whole-number values. These are usually quantities, e.g. the number of shrimp in a stream.
  - **Ordered variables** – have relative values, e.g. 'small', 'medium' or 'large'.

N.B. Numerical values, such as continuous variables, tend to be more informative than ordered and categoric variables.

An investigation tries to find out whether an **observed** link between two variables is…

- **causal** – a change in one variable causes a change in the other, e.g. the more cigarettes you smoke, the greater the chance that you will develop lung cancer.
- **due to association** – the changes in the two variables are linked by a third variable, e.g. as grassland decreases, the number of predators decreases (caused by a third variable, i.e. the number of prey decreasing).
- **due to chance** – the change in the two variables is unrelated; it is coincidental, e.g. people who eat more cheese than others watch more television.

Controlling Variables

In a **fair test,** the only factor that should affect the dependent variable is the independent variable. Other **outside variables** that could influence the results are kept the same (control variables) or eliminated.

It's a lot easier to control all the other variables in a laboratory than in the field, where conditions can't always be controlled. The impact of an outside variable (e.g. light intensity or rainfall) has to be reduced by ensuring all the measurements are affected by it in the same way. For example, all the measurements should be taken at the same time of day.

Control groups are often used in biological and medical research to make sure that any observed results are due to changes in the independent variable only.

A sample is chosen that 'matches' the test group as closely as possible except for the variable that is being investigated, e.g. testing the effect of a drug on reducing blood pressure. The control group must be the same age, gender, have similar diets, lifestyles, blood pressure, general health, etc.

How Science Works Overview

Accuracy and Precision

How accurate data needs to be depends on what the investigation is trying to find out. For example, when measuring the volume of acid needed to neutralise an alkaline solution it is important that equipment is used that is able to accurately measure volumes of liquids.

The data collected must be **precise** enough to form a **valid conclusion**: it should provide clear evidence for or against the hypothesis.

Measurements

Apart from control variables, there are a number of factors that can affect the reliability and validity of measurements:

- **Accuracy of instruments** – depends on how accurately the instrument has been calibrated. An accurate measurement is one that is close to the true value.
- **Resolution (or sensitivity) of instruments** – determined by the smallest change in value that the instrument can detect. The more sensitive the instrument, the more **precise** the value. For example, bathroom scales aren't sensitive enough to detect changes in a baby's weight, but the scales used by a midwife are.
- **Human error** – even if an instrument is used correctly, human error can produce random differences in repeated readings or a systematic shift from the true value if you lose concentration or make the same mistake repeatedly.
- **Systematic error** – can result from repeatedly carrying out the process inconsistently, making the same mistake each time.
- **Random error** – can result from carrying out a process incorrectly on odd occasions or by fluctuations in a reading. The smaller the random error the greater the precision of the reading.

To ensure data is as accurate as possible, you can…

- calculate the **mean** (average) of a set of repeated measurements to reduce the effect of random errors
- increase the number of measurements taken to improve the reliability of the mean / spot anomalies.

Preliminary Investigations

A trial run of an investigation will help identify appropriate values to be recorded, such as the number of repeated readings needed and their range and interval.

You need to examine any **anomalous** (irregular) values to try to determine why they appear. If they have been caused by an equipment failure or human error, it is common practice to ignore them from any calculations.

There will always be some variation in the actual value of a variable, no matter how hard we try to repeat an event.

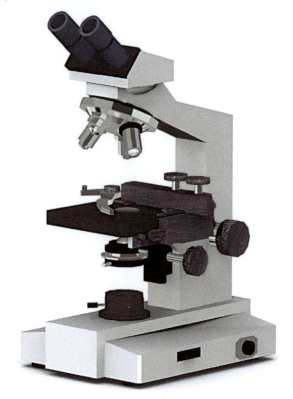

Presenting Data

Data is often presented in a **chart** or **graph** because it makes…

- any patterns more obvious
- it easier to see the relationship between two variables.

The **mean** (or average) of data is calculated by adding all the measurements together, then dividing by the number of measurements taken:

$$\text{Mean} = \frac{\text{Sum of all Values}}{\text{Number of Values}}$$

If you present data clearly, it is easier to identify any anomalous (irregular) values. The type of chart or graph you use to present data depends on the type of variable involved:

1 **Tables** organise data (but patterns and anomalies aren't always obvious)

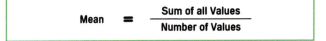

Height of student (cm)	127	165	149	147	155	161	154	138	145
Shoe Size	5	8	5	6	5	5	6	4	5

2 **Bar charts** display data when the independent variable is categoric or discrete and the dependent variable is continuous.

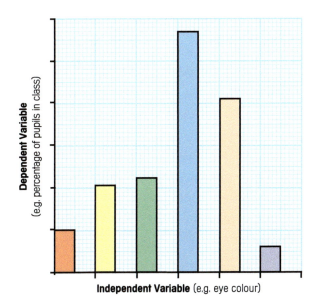

Dependent Variable (e.g. percentage of pupils in class)

Independent Variable (e.g. eye colour)

3 **Line graphs** display data when both variables are continuous.

- Points are joined by straight lines if you don't have data to support the values between the points.
- A line of best fit is drawn if there is sufficient data or if a trend can be assumed.

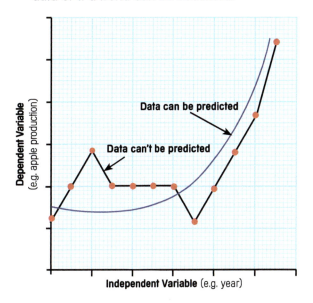

Data can be predicted

Data can't be predicted

Dependent Variable (e.g. apple production)

Independent Variable (e.g. year)

4 **Scattergrams** (scatter diagrams) show the underlying relationship between two variables. This can be made clearer if you include a **line of best fit**. A line of best fit could be a straight line or a smooth curve.

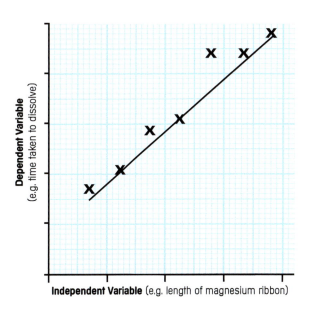

Dependent Variable (e.g. time taken to dissolve)

Independent Variable (e.g. length of magnesium ribbon)

How Science Works Overview

Conclusions **should**…
- describe patterns and relationships between variables
- take all the data into account
- make direct reference to the original hypothesis or prediction
- try to explain the results / observations by making reference to the hypothesis as appropriate.

Conclusions **should not**…
- be influenced by anything other than the data collected (i.e. be biased)
- disregard any data (except anomalous values)
- include any unreasoned speculation.

An **evaluation** looks at the whole investigation. It should consider…
- the original purpose of the investigation
- the appropriateness of the methods and techniques used
- the reliability and validity of the data
- the validity of the conclusions.

The **reliability** of an investigation can be increased by…
- looking at relevant data from secondary sources (i.e. sources created by someone who did not experience first hand or participate in the original experiment)
- using an alternative method to check results
- ensuring results can be reproduced by others.

Science and Society

Scientific understanding can lead to technological developments. These developments can be exploited by different groups of people for different reasons. For example, the successful development of a new drug…
- benefits the drugs company financially
- improves the quality of life for patients
- can benefit society (e.g. if a new drug works, then maybe fewer people will be in hospital, which reduces time off sick, cost to the NHS, etc).

Scientific developments can raise certain **issues**. An issue is an important question that is in dispute and needs to be settled. The resolution of an issue may not be based on scientific evidence alone.

There are several different types of **issue** that can arise:
- **Social** – the impact on the human population of a community, city, country, or the world.
- **Economic** – money and related factors like employment and the distribution of resources.
- **Environmental** – the impact on the planet, its natural ecosystems and resources.
- **Ethical** – what is morally right and wrong; requires a value judgement to be made.

N.B. There is often an overlap between social and economic issues.

Peer Review

Peer review is a process of self-regulation involving qualified professional individuals or experts in a particular field who examine the work undertaken critically. The vast majority of peer review methods are designed to maintain standards and provide credibility for the work that has been undertaken. These methods vary depending on the nature of the work and also on the overall purpose behind the review process.

Evaluating Information

It is important to be able to evaluate information relating to social-scientific issues, for both your GCSE course and to help you make informed decisions in life.

When evaluating information…
- make a list of **pluses** (pros)
- make a list of **minuses** (cons)
- consider how each point might **impact on society**.

You also need to consider whether the source of information is reliable and credible. Some important factors to consider are…
- **opinions**
- **bias**
- **weight of evidence**.

Opinions are personal viewpoints. Opinions backed up by valid and reliable evidence carry far more weight than those based on non-scientific ideas.

Opinions of experts can also carry more weight than non-experts.

Information is **biased** if it favours one particular viewpoint without providing a balanced account.

Biased information might include incomplete evidence or try to influence how you interpret the evidence.

Scientific evidence can be given **undue weight** or dismissed too quickly due to…
- political significance (consequence of the evidence could provoke public or political unrest)
- status of the experiment (e.g. if they do not have academic or professional status, experience, authority or reputation).

Limitations of Science

Although science can help us in lots of ways, it can't supply all the answers. We are still finding out about things and developing our scientific knowledge.

There are some questions that science can't answer. These tend to be questions …
- where beliefs, opinions and ethics are important
- where we don't have enough reproducible, repeatable or valid evidence.

Science can often tell us if something **can** be done, and **how** it can be done, but it can't tell us whether it **should** be done.

Decisions are made by individuals and by society on issues relating to science and technology.

B3 Movement of Molecules In and Out of Cells

Dissolved Substances

Dissolved substances move by…
- **diffusion**
- **active transport**.

Osmosis is the **diffusion of water** from a **dilute solution** to a **more concentrated solution** through a **partially permeable membrane**.

The **partially permeable membrane**…
- **allows water** molecules through
- **stops solute** molecules getting through because they are too large.

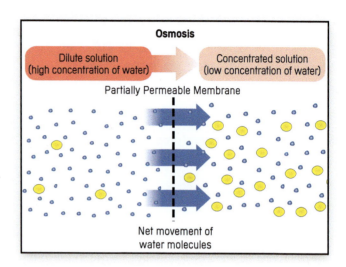

Osmosis

| Dilute solution (high concentration of water) | Concentrated solution (low concentration of water) |

Partially Permeable Membrane

Net movement of water molecules

Osmosis and Cells

When the concentrations of the solutions inside and outside a cell are **different**, it causes water to move into or out of the cell by **osmosis**.

Osmosis will gradually **dilute** the more concentrated solution. For example, water moves from the soil into a plant's root hair cells by osmosis, along a **concentration gradient**.

Less concentrated solution (dilute)

Water

Soil particles

More concentrated solution

Water

Root hair cell

Active Transport

Substances are sometimes absorbed **against** a **concentration gradient**, i.e. in the **opposite direction** to normal distribution. This…
- requires **energy from respiration**
- is known as **active transport**.

Active transport allows cells to absorb **sugar** and **ions**, which can pass through cell membranes, from very **dilute solutions**:
- Plants absorb ions from very dilute solutions in the soil by active transport.
- In humans, sugar can be absorbed from the **intestine** and from the **kidney tubules** by active transport.

Most soft drinks contain water, sugar and ions. Sports drinks contain water, sugars and ions to replace…
- the sugar used to release energy during exercise
- water and ions lost during sweating.

If they are not replaced, the ion and water balance of the body is disturbed and the cells don't work as efficiently.

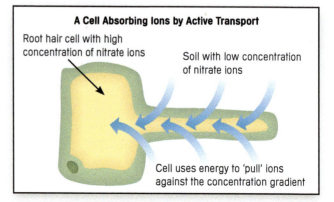

A Cell Absorbing Ions by Active Transport

Root hair cell with high concentration of nitrate ions

Soil with low concentration of nitrate ions

Cell uses energy to 'pull' ions against the concentration gradient

Osmosis • Concentration gradient • Active transport

Exchanging Materials

Many organ systems are **specialised** for exchanging materials. Features that make exchange surfaces efficient include…

- a **large surface area**
- being **thin**, providing a short diffusion path
- having an efficient **blood supply** (in animals)
- being **ventilated** (in animals) for gas exchange.

The **larger and more complex** an organism is, the **more difficult** it is to exchange materials. Exchange surfaces in organisms are **adapted** to maximise their **effectiveness**.

In humans…

- **villi** increase the surface area of the small intestine
- **alveoli** increase the surface area of the lungs.

Villi in the Small Intestine

Villi line the walls of the small intestine. They have…

- a massive **surface area** for exchanging materials across
- an extensive network of blood **capillaries** to absorb the products of digestion by **diffusion** and **active transport.**

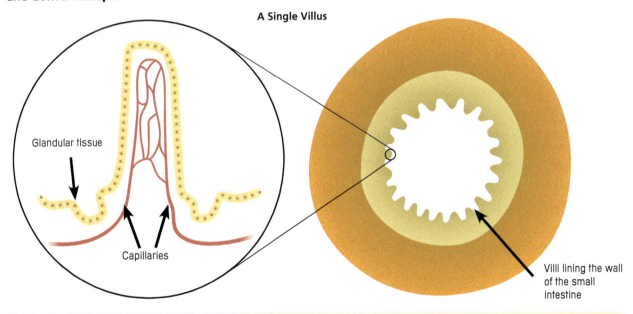

A Single Villus

Glandular tissue

Capillaries

Villi lining the wall of the small intestine

Quick Test

1. What type of molecule is moved by osmosis?
2. What is required for substances to be absorbed against a concentration gradient?
3. How is sugar absorbed through the wall of the small intestine?
4. Name the structure that increases the surface area of…
   a) your intestines
   b) your lungs.
5. In addition to surface area, name one other feature that makes an exchange surface more efficient.

B3 Movement of Molecules In and Out of Cells

The Breathing System

The **breathing system**…
- is located in your thorax (the upper part of your body)
- involves your **lungs**
- is protected by your **ribcage**.

Your thorax is divided from your abdomen by a muscular sheet called the **diaphragm**.

The breathing system takes air into and out of your body so that…
- **oxygen** from the air can **diffuse** into your **blood**
- **carbon dioxide** can **diffuse** from your **blood** into the air.

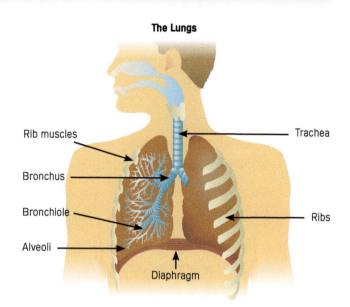

The Lungs

Rib muscles

Bronchus

Bronchiole

Alveoli

Trachea

Ribs

Diaphragm

Alveoli in the Lungs

The air that you breathe in reaches the lungs through the **trachea** (windpipe), which has rings of cartilage to prevent it from collapsing.
- The **trachea** divides into two tubes (the **bronchi**).
- The **bronchi** divide to form **bronchioles**.
- The **bronchioles** divide until they end in air sacs called **alveoli** (there are millions of these).

The alveoli are very close to the blood capillaries. They are efficient at exchanging **oxygen** and **carbon dioxide** because they have…
- a large, moist surface area
- an excellent blood supply.

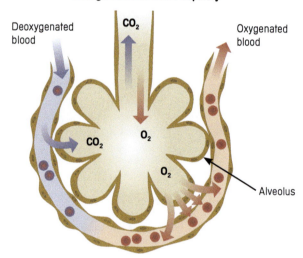

A Single Alveolus and a Capillary

Deoxygenated blood

CO_2

Oxygenated blood

CO_2

O_2

O_2

Alveolus

Ventilation

The movement of air into and out of your lungs is known as **ventilation**.

When you **breathe in** (inhale), your ribcage moves **up** and out and your diaphragm **flattens** (contracts). When you **breathe out** (exhale), your ribcage moves **in** and **down** and your diaphragm moves **up** (relaxes).

Artificial aids for breathing, such as ventilators, have been developed for medical use. They aim to improve gas exchange in the body.

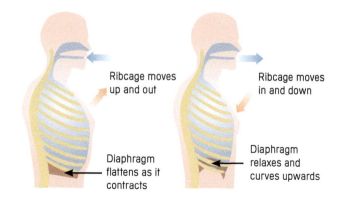

Ribcage moves up and out

Ribcage moves in and down

Diaphragm flattens as it contracts

Diaphragm relaxes and curves upwards

Exchange Systems in Plants

In plants…

- **carbon dioxide** enters **leaves** by **diffusion**
- **water** and **mineral ions** are absorbed by the **roots**.

Roots and leaves are adapted to carry out the exchange of materials:

- **Root hairs** provide a large surface area in roots.
- **Leaves** are broad, thin and flat with lots of internal air spaces to provide the largest surface area possible.

Plants have tiny holes called stomata on the underside of their leaves. During photosynthesis, the stomata…

- let carbon dioxide in (needed for photosynthesis)
- let oxygen out (a product of photosynthesis).

Magnified Cross Section of Leaf

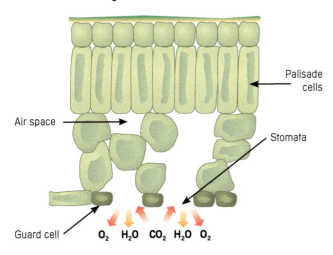

Plants mainly lose water vapour from their leaves. Most of this loss takes place through the stomata. The movement of water through a plant is called transpiration.

Evaporation of water is more rapid in hot, dry and windy conditions.

If plants lose water through the leaves faster than it's replaced by the roots then the stomata can close to prevent **wilting**. But, this means that photosynthesis can't take place.

Evaporation of Water Through Leaves

Cool, damp, not windy

Stomata open allowing transpiration and diffusion of gases

Plant cells full of water so the plant stays erect

Plenty of water in the soil

The surface area of the roots is increased by root hairs

Hot, dry, windy

Stomata close to prevent transpiration. Photosynthesis has to stop

Plant cells short of water so the plant wilts

Not enough water in the soil

The surface area of the roots is increased by root hairs

The size of stomata is controlled by guard cells, which surround them.

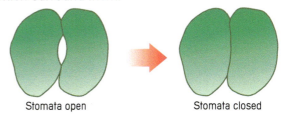

Stomata open

Stomata closed

Quick Test

1. What happens to your ribcage when you breathe in?
2. Where does gas exchange occur in the lungs?
3. Name the process of water movement in plants.
4. Name the cells that open and close stomata.

B3 Transport Systems in Plants and Animals

The Circulatory System

The **circulatory system** transports substances around your body. It consists of your **heart**, your **blood vessels** and your **blood.** Blood is pumped to your lungs so carbon dioxide can be exchanged for oxygen:

- **Oxygenated blood** provides glucose and oxygen to cells.
- **Deoxygenated blood** takes away waste products (including carbon dioxide).

It is a double circulation system. Blood passes through your heart **twice**:

1. To carry blood from your **heart** to your **lungs** then back to your **heart**.
2. To carry blood from your **heart** to all **other organs** then back to your **heart**.

The **right side** of your heart pumps blood that is **low in oxygen** to your **lungs** to pick up oxygen. The **left side** of your heart pumps blood that is **high in oxygen** to all other parts of your **body**.

The heart is the **organ** responsible for continuously pumping blood around your body, so much of its wall is **muscle tissue**. There are four chambers in your heart:

- Left and right atria
- Left and right ventricles.

Blood enters your heart through atria. The atria **contract** and force blood into the ventricles. The ventricles then

Blood Vessels

Arteries	Veins	Capillaries
• Take blood from your heart to your organs. • Have thick walls made from muscle and elastic fibres.	• Take blood from your organs to your heart. • Have thinner walls and valves to prevent backflow.	• Allow substances needed by the cells to pass out of the blood. • Allow substances produced by the cells to pass into the blood. • Are narrow, thin-walled blood vessels.

If arteries begin to narrow and restrict the flow of blood, small mesh tubes called stents are inserted by surgeons to keep them open.

The Blood

Blood is a **tissue** and has four components:
- **Plasma**
- White blood cells
- Red blood cells
- Platelets

Plasma is a straw-coloured liquid that transports…
- **carbon dioxide** from the organs to your lungs
- the soluble products of digestion (e.g. **glucose**) from the small intestine to your organs
- other waste products (e.g. **urea**) from your liver to your kidneys.

Red blood cells…
- transport **oxygen** from your lungs to the organs
- don't have a **nucleus**
- are packed full of the red pigment **haemoglobin**.

In the lungs:

haemoglobin + oxygen ⟶ **oxyhaemoglobin**

In other organs:

oxyhaemoglobin ⟶ haemoglobin + oxygen

The **white blood cells**…
- have a nucleus
- are suspended in the plasma
- form part of your body's defence system against pathogens.

Platelets…
- are small fragments of cells
- don't have a nucleus
- help blood to **clot** if you have a wound.

Artificial blood is being developed as an alternative to blood transfusions. It carries oxygen in situations where a person's red blood cells do not function correctly.

Transport Systems in Plants

Flowering plants have separate transport systems:
- Xylem
- Phloem

Xylem tissue transports **water** and **mineral** ions from roots to the stem and leaves. The movement of water from the roots through the xylem and out of the leaves is called the **transpiration stream**.

Phloem tissue carries **dissolved sugars** from the leaves to the rest of the plant, including the growing regions and the storage organs.

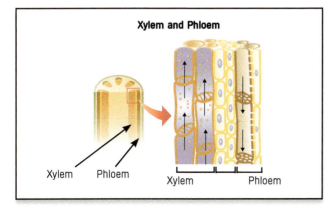

Xylem and Phloem

Xylem   Phloem   Xylem   Phloem

B3 Homeostasis

Homeostasis

Homeostasis means keeping your internal environment constant. It includes monitoring and controlling…
- levels of waste materials
- body temperature
- water and ion content
- blood glucose levels.

Waste Materials

Waste products that have to be removed from the body include:
- **Carbon dioxide**, produced by respiration and removed via the lungs when we breathe out.
- **Urea**, produced in the liver by the breakdown of **amino acids** and removed by the kidneys (in urine). Urine is temporarily stored in the bladder and then excreted as urine.

Body Temperature

Your body temperature should be kept at around 37°C.

The **thermoregulatory centre** in your brain…
- monitors and controls body temperature
- has receptors that monitor the temperature of the blood flowing through the brain
- receives information (impulses) from temperature **receptors** in your skin about the skin's temperature.

Sweating helps to cool your body. When it is hot **more water is lost** by your body, so more water has to be taken in as **drink** or in food to balance this loss.

Skin may appear **flushed** (red) when it's hot. This is due to increased blood flow beneath its surface.

HT Hot Conditions

If core body temperature is too high…
- blood vessels supplying skin capillaries **dilate** (widen) to increase blood flow and heat loss
- sweat glands release more sweat, which cools the skin as it **evaporates**.

HT Cold Conditions

If core body temperature is too low…
- blood vessels supplying skin capillaries **constrict** (narrow) to reduce blood flow and heat loss
- muscles start to '**shiver**' causing heat energy to be released by respiration in cells.

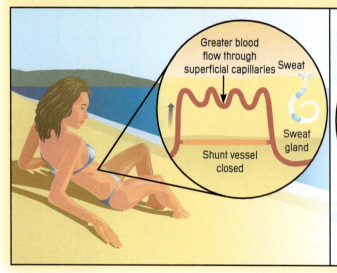

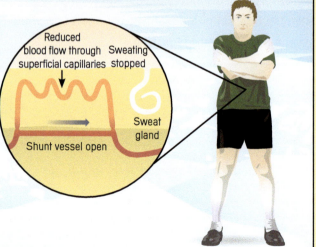

The Kidneys

The kidneys **maintain the concentrations of dissolved substances** in the blood. They…

- regulate the amount of water in the blood
- regulate the amount of **ions** in the blood
- remove all **urea** in the form of **urine**.

Water and ions enter the body when you eat and drink. The level of water and ions needs to be maintained because too much water moving into or out of the cells may damage them.

Blood vessels carry blood through the kidneys where three processes occur:

1. **Ultra filtration** – lots of water and all the small molecules are squeezed out of the blood, under pressure, into tubules in the kidney.
2. **Selective reabsorption** – all the sugar, plus any ions and water needed by the body, are reabsorbed back into the blood from the tubules.
3. **Excretion of waste** – excess water, ions and all of the **urea** now pass to the bladder in the form of urine, where it's stored before being released from the body.

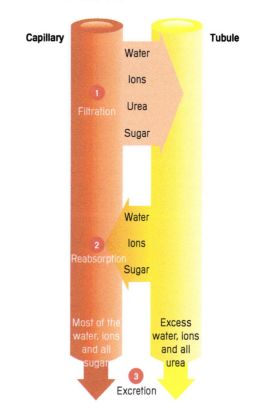

Most people have two **kidneys**, situated on the back wall of the abdomen. When a person's kidneys fail, they may be treated…

- using a **dialysis** machine
- by having a kidney transplant.

Dialysis Machines

As blood flows through a dialysis machine:

1. The blood is separated from the dialysis fluid by **partially permeable membranes**.
2. The membranes allow urea, and any excess substances, to pass from the blood into the dialysis fluid.
3. Concentrations of dissolved substances in the blood are restored to their normal levels.

Dialysis fluid contains the same concentration of useful substances as blood. This ensures **glucose** and essential **mineral ions** aren't lost through diffusion.

Dialysis must be carried out at regular intervals to maintain the patient's health.

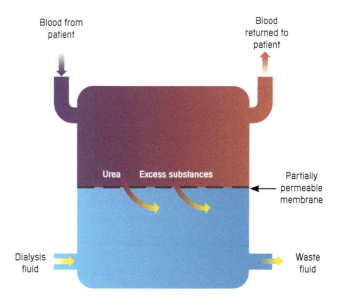

B3 Homeostasis

Kidney Transplants

A kidney transplant involves an individual with two diseased kidneys being given a healthy one from a donor. But, the donor kidney may be **rejected** by the recipient's immune system unless precautions are taken.

There are **antigens** (proteins) on the surface of cells. The recipient's **antibodies** may attack the antigens on the donor organ because they don't recognise them as being part of the recipient's own body.

To prevent rejection of the transplanted kidney:

1. A donor kidney with a '**tissue-type**' similar to that of the recipient is used (this is best achieved if the donor is a close relative).
2. The recipient is treated with drugs that suppress the immune system.

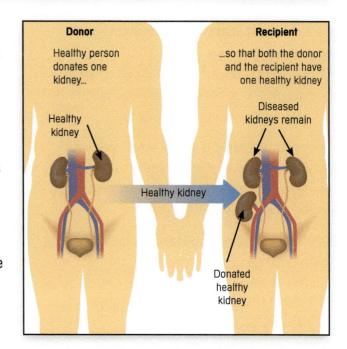

Donor

Healthy person donates one kidney...

Healthy kidney

Recipient

...so that both the donor and the recipient have one healthy kidney

Diseased kidneys remain

Healthy kidney

Donated healthy kidney

Blood Sugar Concentration

The pancreas monitors and controls blood sugar levels and secretes the hormone **insulin**. Insulin allows glucose to move from the blood into the cells.

HT Insulin converts glucose into **glycogen**, which is stored in the liver. A second hormone called **glucagon** is made in the pancreas when blood glucose levels fall too low. This causes glycogen to be converted into glucose and be released into the blood.

$$\text{glucose} \underset{\text{Glucagon}}{\overset{\text{Insulin}}{\rightleftharpoons}} \text{glycogen}$$

The level of insulin in the pancreas affects what happens in the **liver**. If the pancreas doesn't produce enough insulin, a person's blood glucose concentration may rise to a high level. This is a condition called **Type 1 diabetes**. It can be controlled by...

- careful management of **diet** and exercise
- **injecting insulin** into the blood.

Instead of using animal insulin, human insulin is now made (via genetic engineering) quickly and cheaply using bacteria.

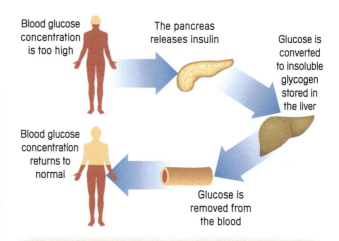

Blood glucose concentration is too high

The pancreas releases insulin

Glucose is converted to insoluble glycogen stored in the liver

Blood glucose concentration returns to normal

Glucose is removed from the blood

Quick Test

1. Which part of the brain monitors body temperature?
2. Where is insulin made?
3. What is urea?
4. Where is urine stored?
5. If a person's kidney fails, what type of machine can be used to filter their blood?
6. What is the main problem with kidney transplants?

The Population Explosion

The **human population** is **growing** exponentially (i.e. with fast growth) and the standard of living for most people has improved a lot over the past 50 years.

This means that…

- raw materials, including non-renewable energy **resources** are being used up quickly
- more and more **waste** is being produced (so more landfill sites are needed)
- improper handling of waste is causing pollution
- there is less land available for plants and animals due to…
  - farming
  - quarrying
  - building
  - dumping waste.

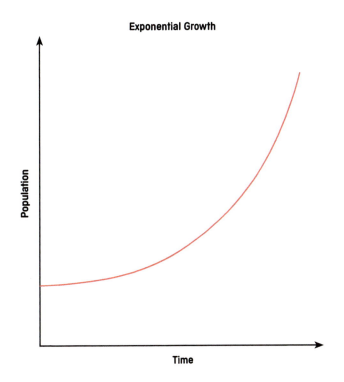

Exponential Growth

Pollution

Waste produced by human activity may pollute…

- **water** – with sewage, fertilisers or toxic chemicals
- **air** – with smoke and gases, e.g. carbon dioxide, which contributes to global warming, and sulfur dioxide and oxides of nitrogen, which contribute to acid rain
- **land** – with toxic chemicals like pesticides and herbicides, which may be washed from land into waterways.

Unless waste is properly handled and stored, more pollution will be caused.

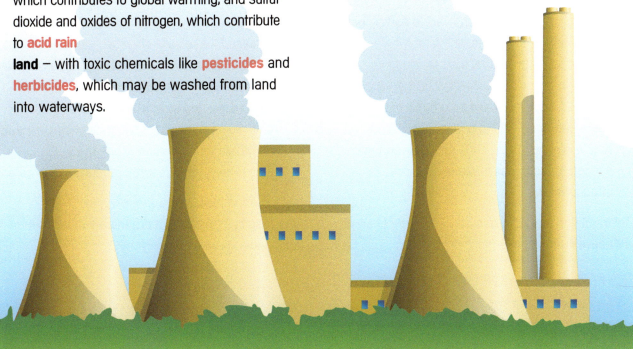

B3 Humans and their Environment

Global Warming

The **greenhouse effect** describes how gases in the atmosphere, such as **methane** (CH_4) and carbon dioxide (CO_2), prevent excess heat from 'escaping' from the Earth's surface into Space.

The levels of these gases are slowly rising. This is because larger quantities are being released into the atmosphere due to…
- the increase in cattle and rice fields (methane)
- the burning of chopped-down wood and industrial burning (carbon dioxide).

As a result, more heat is radiated back to Earth. This is causing **global warming**.

A rise in the Earth's temperature by only a few degrees Celsius could lead to…
- significant climate change
- a rise in sea level
- reduced biodiversity
- changes in migration patterns, e.g. in birds
- changes in the distribution of species.

Carbon dioxide can be **sequestered** in oceans, lakes and ponds. This means CO_2 is taken from the atmosphere and stored in the water. This is an important factor in removing carbon dioxide from the atmosphere.

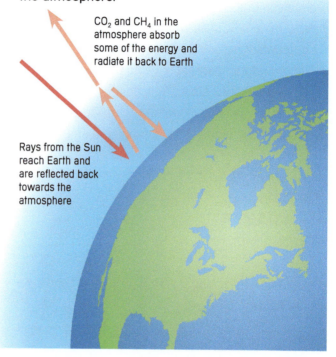

CO_2 and CH_4 in the atmosphere absorb some of the energy and radiate it back to Earth

Rays from the Sun reach Earth and are reflected back towards the atmosphere

Deforestation

Deforestation involves the large-scale cutting down of trees for timber and to provide land for agricultural use. Agricultural land created by deforestation is used for…
- crops for **biofuels** based on ethanol
- cattle and rice fields to provide more food (these organisms produce methane and this has led to increases in methane in the atmosphere).

Deforestation has occurred in many **tropical areas** with devastating consequences for the environment.

Deforestation has…
- **increased** the release of carbon dioxide (CO_2) **into the atmosphere** through burning and the decay of wood by microorganisms
- **reduced** the rate at which carbon dioxide is removed from the atmosphere by **photosynthesis**
- **increased** the amount of **methane** in the atmosphere (produced by organisms like cattle).

Loss of forest leads to a reduction in **biodiversity** and results in the loss of organisms that could be of use in the future.

Destruction of Areas of Peat

The destruction of **peat** bogs and other areas of peat releases carbon dioxide into the atmosphere.

Using peat-free composts could help to reduce this problem.

Key Words   Greenhouse effect • Global warming • Sequestered • Deforestation • Biodiversity • Peat

Biofuels

Many different **microorganisms** (e.g. bacteria or yeast) are involved in the digestion of waste materials. Microorganisms can be used to produce fuels (**biofuels**) from natural products by a form of anaerobic respiration, also known as **fermentation**. All oxygen must be excluded for this to happen.

Biogas, which is mainly **methane**, can be produced in this way from a wide range of plant products and waste materials containing **carbohydrate**.

Waste from sugar factories or sewage works can be used to provide biogas on a large scale.

Large-scale biogas generators are often located near sewage works or sugar factories where the waste can be easily transported. This cuts down on costs.

Smaller biogas generators can supply the energy needs of individual families or farms. Waste is usually collected from kitchens and livestock, and is then digested by bacteria to produce biogas.

These generators usually make enough gas for a small village or a family. The gas is used for cooking on simple stoves and for heating and lighting homes.

Home Biogas System

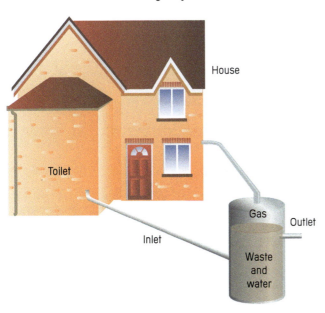

Producing biogas depends on the…
- temperature of the generator
- rate of fermentation
- type of waste used.

There are several designs for biogas generators, but they all need the following:
- A way of putting in the waste material.
- A way of removing the digested waste material.
- A way of removing the biogas and transporting it to where it's needed.

A Simple Biogas Generator

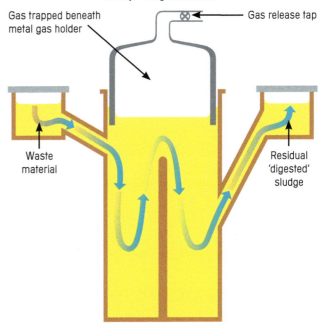

Quick Test

1. Describe how the human population is increasing.
2. List four reasons why there is less land available for plants and animals.
3. What can pollutant gases such as sulfur dioxide cause?
4. Give one reason why deforestation is occurring.
5. Explain the effect that deforestation has on the amount of carbon dioxide in the atmosphere and why?

Food Production

At each stage in a food chain, less material and less energy are contained in the **biomass** of the organisms.

This means it is **more efficient** to produce food from **plants** (rather than animals) because plants are at the beginning of the food chain.

Producing food can be made more efficient by…
- **reducing** the number of stages in the food chain
- restricting the energy lost by livestock.

But, consumers are becoming more conscious of the ethical, environmental and economic implications of how we produce our food.

Intensive Farming

Some livestock are **intensively farmed**. This involves animals such as chickens or pigs being housed close together in indoor pens.

Advantages of Intensive Farming

- Accommodation can be cheap and secure from predators, e.g. foxes.
- Environmental conditions can be controlled, e.g. light and temperature.
- Energy isn't wasted on movement or heat, making energy transfer efficient.
- Cheap product for the farmer to sell.

Disadvantages of Intensive Farming

- Disease can spread very quickly in crowded conditions. Sometimes this means that expensive antibiotics must be used at a cost to the farmer.
- Behaviour of animals can cause them to fight with each other leaving some animals injured or even dead.
- Animal welfare standards may not be met. Some people consider intensive farming to be cruel.
- Environmental conditions are controlled by using equipment that relies on burning fossil fuels, e.g. generating electricity for heaters or lights.

Sustainable Food Production

Sustainable **food production** uses methods that…
- allow food to be produced for consumption now
- **conserve** resources so that food can continue to be produced in the same way by future generations.

Example − fish stocks

The UK has one of the largest sea fishing industries, but fish stocks in the oceans are declining.

To ensure the industry can continue and fish stocks can be conserved, quotas are set to prevent over-fishing:
- The mesh size of nets has been increased to prevent young fish being caught before they **reach breeding age**.
- **Quotas** for different types of fish are put in place to control the amount caught, so that a breeding population is maintained.

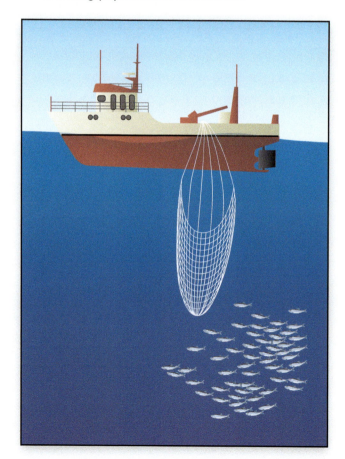

Food Miles

The distances that food travels from where it is grown to where it is bought are called **food miles**.

Where product is grown → **Packaging factory** → **Distribution depot** → **Supermarket** → **Home**

Consumers are increasingly concerned about **food miles** because of their environmental affect:

1. The burning of fossil fuels commonly provides the fuel for transporting food.
2. Burning fossil fuels increases the amount of carbon dioxide in the atmosphere.

You can help to reduce your food miles by buying products grown…

- in Britain
- locally or from farmers' markets.

Mycoprotein

Mycoprotein is a protein-rich food suitable for vegetarians made by using *Fusarium*, a type of **fungus**.

The fungus grows…

- in a fermenter
- on glucose syrup
- in **aerobic** conditions.

The biomass is harvested and purified to produce mycoprotein.

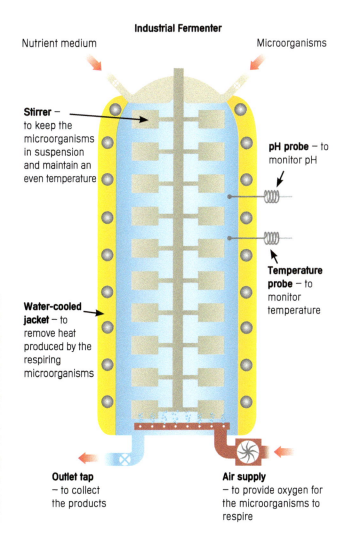

Industrial Fermenter

Nutrient medium

Microorganisms

Stirrer – to keep the microorganisms in suspension and maintain an even temperature

pH probe – to monitor pH

Temperature probe – to monitor temperature

Water-cooled jacket – to remove heat produced by the respiring microorganisms

Outlet tap – to collect the products

Air supply – to provide oxygen for the microorganisms to respire

Quick Test

1. What process produces fuels from natural products?
2. What does biogas largely consist of?
3. Give two reasons why amounts of greenhouse gases are increasing in the atmosphere.
4. What type of microorganism produces a protein-rich food?
5. How are fishermen conserving stocks of fish?

B3 Exam Practice Questions

1 Katie wanted to investigate osmosis. She cut five equal size potato chips, placed them into five different sugar solutions and left them for 24 hours. She measured the mass of the potato chip before and after the investigation. Her results are shown in the table.

Concentration of Sugar Solution (M)	Mass of Potato Chip Before (g)	Mass of Potato Chip After (g)	Difference in Mass (g)
0	1.62	1.74	0.12
0.25	1.72	1.62	0.10
0.50	1.69	1.62	0.07
0.75	1.76	1.60	0.16
1	1.74	1.59	0.15

a) What is the independent variable in the investigation?

.... **(1 mark)**

b) Name a variable that should be kept constant during the investigation.

.... **(1 mark)**

c) In which concentration did the potato gain mass?

.... **(1 mark)**

d) What caused this gain in mass?

.... **(1 mark)**

e) How could the student increase the reliability of her results?

.... **1 mark)**

2 State two differences between active transport and diffusion.

....

.... **(2 marks)**

3 Explain how the small intestine has adapted to become efficient at absorbing digested food molecules.

....

.... **(2 marks)**

4 The diagram below shows some of the structures in the thorax.

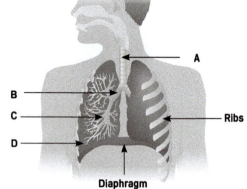

a) Name the structures A, B, C and D. **(4 marks)**

A ....

B ....

C ....

D ....

b) Alveoli are adapted to help gas exchange in the lungs.

    i) Which gas diffuses from the blood into the alveoli? .... **(1 mark)**

    ii) Which gas diffuses from the alveoli into the blood? .... **(1 mark)**

5 Circle the correct options. Which of the following are most likely to be true? When the stomata are open, the leaf is...

absorbing oxygen　　　　　**giving off water vapour**　　　　　**absorbing carbon dioxide**

giving off carbon dioxide　　　**giving off oxygen**　　　　　　**absorbing water**　　　**(3 marks)**

6 Fill in the missing words.

Oxygenated blood from the .... returns to the left atrium of the heart in the pulmonary

.... From here it enters the left ventricle and leaves the heart in the aorta to go to

the .... From the body, ... blood returns via the vena cava to the

right atrium and then leaves the heart in the pulmonary artery to go to the lungs.　　　**(4 marks)**

7 Name the transport system in plants that moves water and mineral ions from the roots to the stem and leaves.

.... **(1 mark)**

8 The human population is ever expanding, which increases pressure on the environment and Earth's resources.

a) What term involves the large-scale cutting down of trees for timber or to provide land for agricultural use?

.... **(1 mark)**

b) List one effect that this can have on the environment.

.... **(1 mark)**

9 As we are running out of non-renewable energy resources scientists are looking for different ways to generate energy. What type of reaction produces the biogas methane?

.... **(1 mark)**

HT **10** **a)** Complete the following sentence by selecting the correct words.

	more concentrated and lighter in colour.
In hot weather the urine becomes...	more concentrated and darker in colour.
	less concentrated and lighter in colour. **(1 mark)**

    b) Which of the following substances are not found in the urine of a healthy person? Circle the correct options.

      Glucose　　　**Water**　　　**Urea**　　　**Ions**　　　**Protein**　　　　　**(2 marks)**

C3 The Periodic Table

Early Attempts to Classify the Elements

Several attempts have been made to group the **elements** in a table, firstly out of curiosity, then as a useful tool to help scientists and finally as an important summary of the structure of atoms.

When **John Newlands** tried to arrange a periodic table in 1864, only 63 elements were known; many were still **undiscovered**. Newlands arranged the known elements in order of their **atomic mass** and found similar properties amongst every eighth element in the series. This makes sense since the noble gases (Group 8) weren't discovered until 1894.

He noticed **periodicity** (repeated patterns) although the missing elements caused problems.

But, strictly following the order of **atomic mass** created problems because it meant some of the elements were placed in the **wrong group**.

Dimitri Mendeleev realised that some elements had yet to be discovered, so when he created his table in 1869 he left **gaps** to allow for their discovery. He used his periodic table to predict the existence of other elements.

The Modern Periodic Table

The discovery of **subatomic particles** (**protons**, **neutrons** and **electrons**) and **electronic structure** early in the 20th century provided further evidence that could be used to create a table. The Periodic Table was then arranged in order of atomic (proton) numbers. So, the modern Periodic Table is an arrangement of the elements in terms of their **electronic structure**.

The elements are arranged in **periods** (rows) according to the **number of electrons** in their outer **energy level** (shell). From left to right across each period, an energy level is gradually filled with electrons. In the next period, the next energy level is filled, etc.

This arrangement means elements with the same number of electrons in their outer energy level are in the same **group** (column). For example, Group 1 elements have one electron in their outer energy level. Elements that have the **same number of electrons** in their outer energy level have **similar properties**.

The table is called a **Periodic Table** because similar properties occur at **regular intervals**.

1	2											3	4	5	6	7	8 or 0
						1 **H** hydrogen 1											4 **He** helium 2
7 **Li** lithium 3	9 **Be** beryllium 4											11 **B** boron 5	12 **C** carbon 6	14 **N** nitrogen 7	16 **O** oxygen 8	19 **F** fluorine 9	20 **Ne** neon 10
23 **Na** sodium 11	24 **Mg** magnesium 12											27 **Al** aluminium 13	28 **Si** silicon 14	31 **P** phosphorus 15	32 **S** sulfur 16	35.5 **Cl** chlorine 17	40 **Ar** argon 18
39 **K** potassium 19	40 **Ca** calcium 20	45 **Sc** scandium 21	48 **Ti** titanium 22	51 **V** vanadium 23	52 **Cr** chromium 24	55 **Mn** manganese 25	56 **Fe** iron 26	59 **Co** cobalt 27	59 **Ni** nickel 28	63.5 **Cu** copper 29	65 **Zn** zinc 30	70 **Ga** gallium 31	73 **Ge** germanium 32	75 **As** arsenic 33	79 **Se** selenium 34	80 **Br** bromine 35	84 **Kr** krypton 36
85 **Rb** rubidium 37	88 **Sr** strontium 38	89 **Y** yttrium 39	91 **Zr** zirconium 40	93 **Nb** niobium 41	96 **Mo** molybdenum 42	[98] **Tc** technetium 43	101 **Ru** ruthenium 44	103 **Rh** rhodium 45	106 **Pd** palladium 46	108 **Ag** silver 47	112 **Cd** cadmium 48	115 **In** indium 49	119 **Sn** tin 50	122 **Sb** antimony 51	128 **Te** tellurium 52	127 **I** iodine 53	131 **Xe** xenon 54
133 **Cs** caesium 55	137 **Ba** barium 56	139 **La*** lanthanum 57	178 **Hf** hafnium 72	181 **Ta** tantalum 73	184 **W** tungsten 74	186 **Re** rhenium 75	190 **Os** osmium 76	192 **Ir** iridium 77	195 **Pt** platinum 78	197 **Au** gold 79	201 **Hg** mercury 80	204 **Tl** thallium 81	207 **Pb** lead 82	209 **Bi** bismuth 83	[209] **Po** polonium 84	[210] **At** astatine 85	[222] **Rn** radon 86
[223] **Fr** francium 87	[226] **Ra** radium 88	[227] **Ac*** actinium 89	[261] **Rf** rutherfordium 104	[262] **Db** dubnium 105	[266] **Sg** seaborgium 106	[264] **Bh** bohrium 107	[277] **Hs** hassium 108	[268] **Mt** meitnerium 109	[271] **Ds** darmstadtium 110	[272] **Rg** roentgenium 111							

Key Words   Element • Proton • Neutron • Electron • Electronic structure

Group 1 – The Alkali Metals

There are six elements in **Group 1**. They are known as the **alkali metals**.

Alkali metals…
- have **low** melting and boiling points that **decrease** as you go down the group
- have a **low** density (lithium, sodium and potassium are less dense than water)
- become **more reactive** as you go down the group.

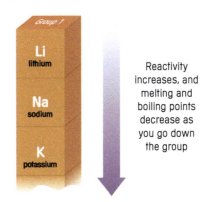

Reactivity increases, and melting and boiling points decrease as you go down the group

Trends in Group 1

Alkali metals have **similar properties** to each other because they have the same number of electrons in their outer energy level, i.e. the highest occupied energy level in an atom of each element contains **one electron**.

Alkali metals become **more reactive** as you go down the group because the outer energy level gets further away from the influence of the nucleus, and so an **electron is lost more easily**.

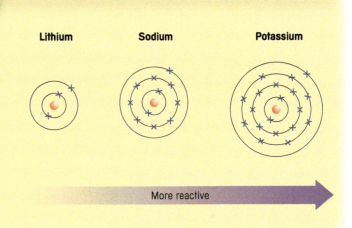

Lithium   Sodium   Potassium

More reactive

Reactions of Alkali Metals

The alkali metals are stored under oil because they react very vigorously with oxygen and water. When alkali metals react with **water**, a **metal hydroxide** is formed and **hydrogen** gas is given off. For example…

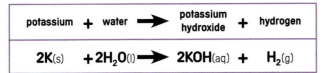

potassium + water ⟶	potassium hydroxide + hydrogen
$2K_{(s)} + 2H_2O_{(l)} \rightarrow$	$2KOH_{(aq)} + H_{2(g)}$

If a metal hydroxide (e.g. potassium hydroxide) is **dissolved** in water, an **alkaline solution** is produced.

Alkali metals react with **non-metals** to form **ionic compounds**. When this happens, the metal atom **loses** one electron to form a metal ion with a **positive charge** (+1). The products are **white solids** that **dissolve** in water to form **colourless** solutions.

Alkali Metals Reacting with Water

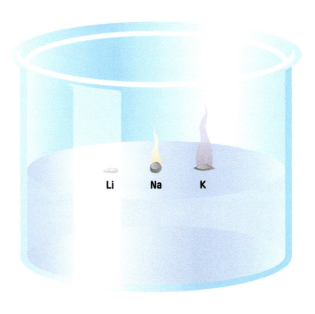

Li   Na   K

Key Words   Alkali metal • Ionic compound   **29**

C3 The Periodic Table

Group 7 – The Halogens

There are five **elements** in Group 7. They are known as the **halogens**. They are non-metals.

The halogens…
- have melting and boiling points that **increase** as you go down the group (at room temperature, fluorine and chlorine are gases, and bromine is a liquid)
- have **coloured vapours** (chlorine's and bromine's vapours smell particularly strong)
- exist as **molecules** made up of **pairs of atoms**
- become **less reactive** as you go down the group.

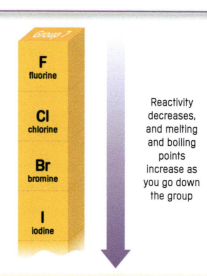

Reactivity decreases, and melting and boiling points increase as you go down the group

HT Trends in Group 7

Halogens have **similar properties** because they have the same number of electrons (i.e. seven) in their outer energy level.

They become less reactive as you go down the group because the outer energy level gets further away from the influence of the nucleus, and so an electron **is gained less easily**.

The more energy levels an atom has…
- the more easily electrons are lost
- the less easily electrons are gained.

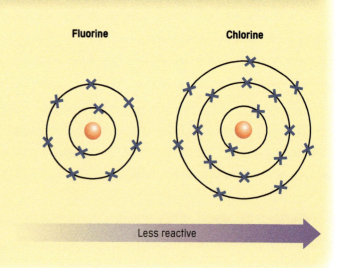

Fluorine   Chlorine

Less reactive

Reactions of Halogens

Halogens react with **metals** to produce **ionic salts**. The **halogen atom gains** one electron to form a **halide ion** (i.e. a chloride, bromide or iodide ion) that carries a **negative charge** (-1). For example:

lithium	+	chlorine	➔	lithium chloride
2Li(s)	+	**Cl₂**(g)	➔	**2LiCl**(s)

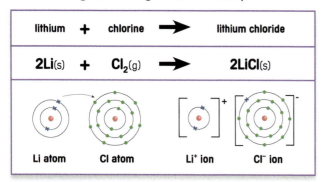

Li atom   Cl atom   Li⁺ ion   Cl⁻ ion

Halogens react with other **non-metallic** elements to form **molecular compounds**. For example:

hydrogen	+	chlorine	➔	hydrogen chloride
H₂(g)	+	**Cl₂**(g)	➔	**2HCl**(g)

A more reactive halogen will **displace** a less reactive halogen from an aqueous solution of its salt, i.e.…
- chlorine will displace both bromine and iodine
- bromine will displace iodine.

The Transition Metals

In the **centre** of the Periodic Table, between Groups 2 and 3, is a block of metallic elements called the **transition metals** (or **transition elements**).

Many transition metals…

- form **coloured compounds**
- have **ions** with **different charges**, e.g. Fe^{2+} and Fe^{3+}
- can be used as catalysts to speed up chemical reactions.

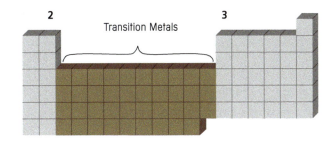

Transition Metals

Properties of Transition Metals

Like all other metals, transition metals…
- are good **conductors** of heat and electricity
- can be **easily bent** or **hammered** into shape.

In comparison to Group 1 metals, transition metals…
- have higher densities and higher melting points (except mercury, which is liquid at room temperature)
- are harder and more mechanically strong (except mercury)
- are much **less reactive** and don't react as vigorously with oxygen or water.

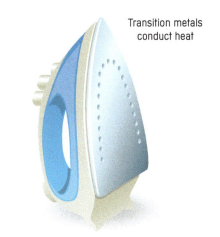

Transition metals conduct heat

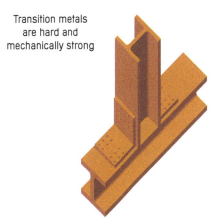

Transition metals are hard and mechanically strong

Transition metals can be bent

Quick Test

1 How did Newlands, and then Mendeleev attempt to classify the elements?
2 Upon the discovery of protons, neutrons and electrons, how was the Periodic Table arranged?
3 What gas is produced when lithium reacts with water?
4 Fill in the missing words:
  a) Compared to Group 1 elements, transition metals have _____ melting points, are stronger and _____ and are _____ reactive.
  b) A more reactive halogen can _____ a less reactive halogen from an aqueous solution of its salt.

C3 Water

Drinking Water

Water of the correct quality is **essential** for **life**. Water naturally contains **microorganisms** and **dissolved salts**, which should be of sufficiently low levels to be safe for humans to drink.

Water that is good quality and safe to drink is produced in the following way:

1. The water is passed through a **filter bed** to remove any solid particles.
2. **Chlorine gas** is then added to kill any harmful microorganisms.
3. **Fluoride** is added to drinking water in order to reduce tooth decay (although too much fluoride can cause discolouration of teeth).

To improve the taste and quality of tap water, more dissolved substances can be removed by passing the water through a **filter** containing carbon, silver and **ion exchange resins**.

Any water can be **distilled** to produce **pure water**, i.e. water that contains no dissolved substances. The water is boiled to produce steam, which is condensed by cooling it to produce pure liquid water. This process uses a lot of energy, which makes distillation an expensive process.

Hard and Soft Water

The amount of compounds present in tap water determines whether it's described as **hard** or **soft**.

Soft water doesn't contain many dissolved compounds so it readily forms a **lather** with soap. Permanently hard water remains hard upon boiling. Temporary hard water is softened upon boiling.

Most **hard water** contains calcium or magnesium compounds that dissolve in natural water as it flows over ground or rocks containing compounds of these elements. These dissolved substances react with soap to form **scum**, which makes it harder to form a lather. Soapless detergents do not form scum.

HT Temporary hard water contains hydrogencarbonate ions (HCO_3^-) that decompose upon heating to produce carbonate (CO_3^{2-}) ions. These carbonate ions react with calcium and/or magnesium ions to form precipitates.

Advantage of hard water:
- The dissolved compounds in water are **good for your health**, e.g. calcium compounds help the development of strong bones and teeth, and also help to reduce the risk of heart diseases.

Disadvantages of hard water:
- More soap is needed to form a lather, which increases costs.
- Using hard water often leads to deposits (called scale) forming in heating systems and appliances like kettles, which **reduces** their **efficiency**.

Removing Hardness

To make hard water soft, the **dissolved** calcium and magnesium **ions** need to be removed. This can be done in one of two ways:
- Add **sodium carbonate solution** (washing soda) to it. The carbonate ions react with the calcium and magnesium ions to form calcium carbonate and magnesium carbonate (respectively), which precipitate out of solution as they are both insoluble.
- Pass the hard water through an **ion-exchange column**, which contains hydrogen ions or sodium ions. As the hard water passes through the column, the calcium and magnesium ions contained in it are replaced by hydrogen or sodium ions.

Ion • Distillation • Efficiency

Measuring Energy by Calorimetry

The unit of measurement for **energy** is the **joule** (**J**). It takes 4.2 joules of energy to heat up 1g of water by 1°C. This amount of energy is called 1 **calorie** (**cal**), i.e. 1 calorie = 4.2 joules.

Information about the energy provided by food products is given in kilocalories (kcal). When any **chemical change** takes place it is accompanied by an **energy change**, i.e. energy can be taken in or given out. The relative amounts of energy produced by food or fuels can be measured using **calorimetry**.

To measure the temperature change that takes place when a fuel burns, follow this method:

1. Place 100g of water in a calorimeter (a container made of glass or metal) and measure the temperature of the water.
2. Find the mass (in grams) of the fuel to be burned.
3. Burn the fuel under the water in the calorimeter for a few minutes.
4. Record the new temperature and calculate the temperature change of the water.

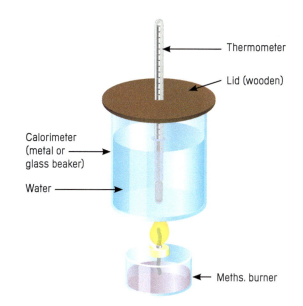

5. Weigh the fuel and calculate how much fuel has been used.
6. The energy released (Q) can be calculated by using the following formula:

$$Q = mc\Delta T$$

where m is the mass of water being heated, c is 4.2 (a constant) and ΔT is the temperature change

Making and Breaking Bonds

In a chemical reaction, new substances are produced. In order to do this, the **bonds** in the reactants must be **broken** and new bonds are **made** to form the products.

Breaking a chemical bond requires a lot of energy – this is an **endothermic** process.

When a new chemical bond is **formed**, energy is given out – this is an **exothermic** process.

HT If more energy is required to break old bonds than is released when the new bonds are formed, the reaction must be **endothermic**.

If more energy is released when the new bonds are formed than is needed to break the old bonds, the reaction must be **exothermic**.

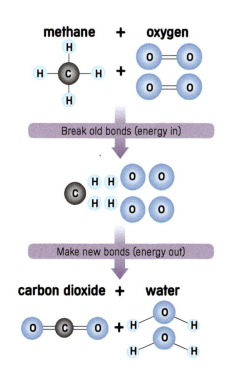

C3 Calculating and Explaining Energy Change

Measuring Energy of Chemical Reactions

The amount of energy produced in a **chemical reaction** in solution can be measured by mixing the reactants in an **insulated** container. This enables the temperature change to be measured before heat is lost to the surroundings. This method would be suitable for **neutralisation** reactions and reactions involving solids, e.g. zinc and acid.

HT Energy Calculations

Example: Calculate the energy transferred in the following reaction:

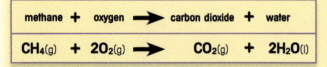

methane	+	oxygen	⟶	carbon dioxide	+	water
$CH_{4(g)}$	+	$2O_{2(g)}$	⟶	$CO_{2(g)}$	+	$2H_2O_{(l)}$

Bond energies needed for this are:
C–H is 412kJ/mol, O=O is 496kJ/mol,
C=O is 805kJ/mol, H–O is 463kJ/mol

Energy used to break bonds is:
4 C–H = 4 x 412 = 1648kJ, 2 O=O = 2 x 496 = 992kJ
Total = 1648kJ + 992kJ = **2640kJ**

Energy given out by making bonds:
2 C=O = 2 x 805 = 1610kJ
4 H–O = 4 x 463 = 1852kJ
Total = 1610kJ + 1852kJ = **3462kJ**

Energy change (ΔH) = Energy used to break bonds – Energy given out by making bonds

= 2640kJ – 3462kJ = **–822kJ**

Energy Level Diagrams

The energy changes in a chemical reaction can be illustrated using an **energy level diagram**:

1 In an **exothermic** reaction, energy is given out. This means energy is being lost, so the products have less energy than the reactants.

2 In an **endothermic** reaction, energy is being taken in. This means that energy is being gained, so the products have more energy than the reactants.

3 The **activation energy** is the energy needed to start a reaction, i.e. to break the old bonds.

4 **Catalysts** reduce the activation energy needed for a reaction – this makes the reaction go faster.

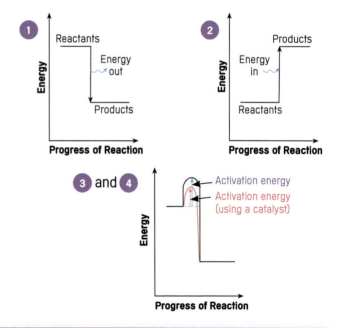

Hydrogen as a Fuel

Hydrogen can be used...

- as a fuel in combustion engines

hydrogen	+	oxygen	⟶	water	+	heat

- in fuel cells, which produce electricity that can be used to power vehicles.

Fuel cells are very efficient and produce less pollution than fossil fuels, but to make the hydrogen fuel, energy is needed, which may come from fossil fuels.

Flame Tests

Flame tests can be used to identify metal **ions**.

Lithium, sodium, potassium, calcium and barium compounds can be recognised by the distinctive colours they produce in a **flame test**.

To do a flame test, follow this method:
1. Heat and then dip a piece of nichrome (a nickel-chromium alloy) wire in concentrated hydrochloric acid to clean it.
2. Dip the wire in the compound.
3. Put it into a Bunsen flame. The following distinctive colours indicate the presence of certain ions:
   - Green for **barium**
   - Brick red for **calcium**
   - Crimson red for **lithium**
   - Lilac for **potassium**
   - Yellow for **sodium**.

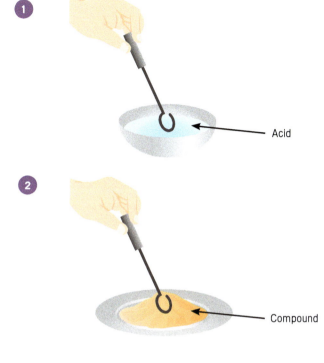

Acid

Compound

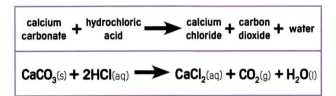

| Barium | Calcium | Lithium | Potassium | Sodium |

Reacting Carbonates with Dilute Acid

Carbonates react with **dilute acids** to form **carbon dioxide** gas (and a salt and water). Carbon dioxide turns limewater milky. For example:

calcium carbonate	+	hydrochloric acid	→	calcium chloride	+	carbon dioxide	+	water

$$CaCO_3(s) + 2HCl(aq) \longrightarrow CaCl_2(aq) + CO_2(g) + H_2O(l)$$

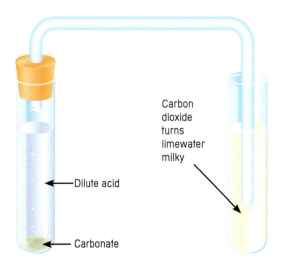

Carbon dioxide turns limewater milky

Dilute acid

Carbonate

C3 Further Analysis and Quantitative Chemistry

Precipitation of Metal Ions

Metal compounds in solution contain **metal ions**. Some of these form **precipitates**, i.e. **insoluble** solids that come out of solution when sodium hydroxide solution is added to them.

For example, when sodium hydroxide solution is added to calcium chloride solution, a white precipitate of calcium hydroxide is formed (as well as sodium chloride solution). You can see how this precipitate is formed by considering the ions involved.

The table below shows the precipitates formed when **metal ions** are mixed with sodium hydroxide solution.

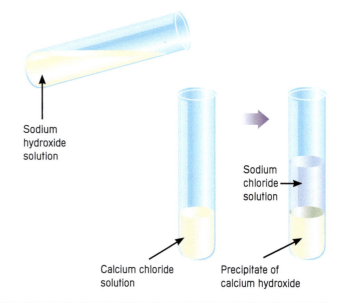

Sodium hydroxide solution

Sodium chloride solution

Calcium chloride solution

Precipitate of calcium hydroxide

Metal Ion		Precipitate Formed	
		Precipitate	Precipitate Colour
Aluminium	$Al^{3+}_{(aq)}$	Aluminium hydroxide	White (dissolves with excess sodium hydroxide)
Calcium	$Ca^{2+}_{(aq)}$	Calcium hydroxide	White
Magnesium	$Mg^{2+}_{(aq)}$	Magnesium hydroxide	White
Copper(II)	$Cu^{2+}_{(aq)}$	Copper(II) hydroxide	Blue
Iron(II)	$Fe^{2+}_{(aq)}$	Iron(II) hydroxide	Green
Iron(III)	$Fe^{3+}_{(aq)}$	Iron(III) hydroxide	Brown

More Examples of Precipitations

If dilute hydrochloric acid and barium chloride solution are added to a solution containing **sulfate ions**, a white precipitate of barium sulfate is produced.

Precipitates with silver nitrate solution can be produced by **halide ions** (chloride, bromide and iodide ions) in solution in the presence of dilute nitric acid:

- Silver chloride is white.
- Silver bromide is cream.
- Silver iodide is yellow.

Quick Test

1. What is produced when hard water reacts with soap?
2. What are the normal units of energy?
3. What happens to energy when bonds are formed?
4. In a flame test, which compound results in a crimson flame?
5. What colour precipitate do calcium ions form with a sodium hydroxide solution?
6. What kind of ions form a blue precipitate with sodium hydroxide solution?
7. What kind of precipitate do chloride ions form with silver nitrate solution in the presence of nitric acid?

Titration

Titration is an accurate technique that you can use to find out **how much** of an **acid** is needed to neutralise an alkali.

When **neutralisation** takes place, the hydrogen ions (H^+) from the acid join with the hydroxide ions (OH^-) from the alkali to form water (neutral pH).

hydrogen ion	+	hydroxide ion	$\rightarrow$	water molecule
$H^+_{(aq)}$	+	$OH^-_{(aq)}$	$\rightarrow$	$H_2O_{(l)}$

Use this titration method:

1. Wash and rinse a pipette with the alkali that you will use.
2. Use the pipette to measure out a known and accurate volume of the alkali.
3. Place the alkali in a clean, dry conical flask. Add a suitable indicator, e.g. phenolphthalein.
4. Place the acid in a burette that has been carefully washed and rinsed with the acid. Take a reading of the volume of acid in the burette (initial reading).
5. Carefully add the acid to the alkali until the indicator changes colour to show neutrality (phenolphthalein turns pink). This is called the **end point**. Take a reading of the volume of acid in the burette (final reading).
6. Calculate the volume of acid added (i.e. subtract the final reading from the initial reading).

This method can be repeated to check results and can then be performed without an indicator in order to obtain the salt.

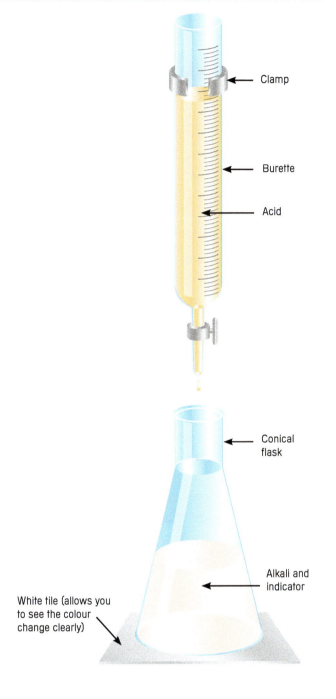

Clamp

Burette

Acid

Conical flask

Alkali and indicator

White tile (allows you to see the colour change clearly)

Indicators

Different strength acids and alkalis can react together to form a neutral solution. You must use a suitable **indicator** in titrations. For example, if you have a strong acid and strong alkali you should use any suitable acid–base indicator (e.g. litmus).

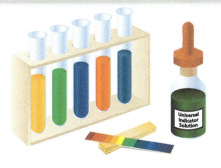

HT Titration

Titration can be used to find the **concentration** of an **acid** or **alkali** providing you know either...

- the relative **volumes** of acid and alkali used **or**
- the **concentration** of the other acid or alkali.

It will help if you break down the calculation:

1. Write down a **balanced equation** for the reaction in order to determine the ratio of moles of acid to alkali involved.

2. Calculate the number of moles in the solution of known volume and concentration. (You will know the number of moles in the other solution from your previous calculation.)

3. Calculate the concentration of the other solution using this formula:

$$\text{Concentration of solution (mol dm}^{-3}\text{ or M)} = \frac{\text{Number of moles of solute (mol)}}{\text{Volume of solution (dm}^{-3}\text{)}}$$

Example 1

A titration is carried out and $0.04dm^3$ hydrochloric acid neutralises $0.08dm^3$ sodium hydroxide of concentration $1mol\ dm^{-3}$. Calculate the concentration of the hydrochloric acid.

Write the balanced symbol equation for the reaction

$$HCl_{(aq)} + NaOH_{(aq)} \rightarrow NaCl_{(aq)} + H_2O_{(l)}$$

You can see that one mole of HCl neutralises one mole of NaOH. So rearrange the formula

$$\text{Number of moles of NaOH} = \text{Concentration of NaOH} \times \text{Volume of NaOH}$$

$$= 1mol\ dm^{-3} \times 0.08dm^3$$

$$= \mathbf{0.08mol}$$

Number of moles of HCl used up in the reaction is also 0.08mol. Now calculate the concentration of HCl

$$\text{Concentration of HCl} = \frac{\text{Number of moles of HCl}}{\text{Volume of HCl}}$$

$$= \frac{0.08mol}{0.04dm^3}$$

$$= \mathbf{2mol\ dm^{-3}}$$

Example 2

A titration is carried out and $0.035dm^3$ sulfuric acid of concentration $0.6mol\ dm^{-3}$ neutralises $0.14dm^3$ sodium hydroxide. Calculate the concentration of the sodium hydroxide.

Write the balanced symbol equation for the reaction

$$H_2SO_{4(aq)} + 2NaOH_{(aq)} \rightarrow Na_2SO_{4(aq)} + 2H_2O_{(l)}$$

This time, one mole of H_2SO_4 neutralises two moles of NaOH

$$\text{Number of moles of }H_2SO_4 = \text{Concentration of }H_2SO_4 \times \text{Volume of }H_2SO_4$$

$$= 0.6mol\ dm^{-3} \times 0.035dm^3$$

$$= \mathbf{0.021mol}$$

Calculate the number of moles of NaOH used up in the reaction. Then calculate the concentration of NaOH

$$\text{No. of moles} = 2 \times 0.021 = \mathbf{0.042mol}$$

$$\text{Concentration of NaOH} = \frac{\text{Number of moles of NaOH}}{\text{Volume of NaOH}}$$

$$= \frac{0.042mol}{0.14dm^3}$$

$$= \mathbf{0.3mol\ dm^{-3}}$$

Quick Test

1. What is the name of the technique used to accurately determine how much acid is needed to neutralise an alkali?
2. Name a suitable indicator for accurately neutralising a strong alkali with a strong acid.
3. What is the concentration of a solution of sodium hydroxide that contains three moles in $4dm^3$?

The Haber Process

Reversible reactions may not go to completion. But they can still be used efficiently in continuous processes such as the **Haber process.**

The Haber process is used to manufacture **ammonia**. The raw materials for this process are…
- **nitrogen** – from the fractional distillation of liquid air
- **hydrogen** – from natural gas and steam.

The purified nitrogen and hydrogen are passed over an **iron catalyst** at a…
- **high temperature** (about 450°C)
- **high pressure** (about 200 atmospheres).

Some of the hydrogen and nitrogen **reacts** to **form ammonia**. The **ammonia** produced can **break down** again into **nitrogen** and **hydrogen**.

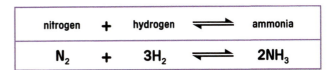

nitrogen	+	hydrogen	⇌	ammonia
N_2	+	$3H_2$	⇌	$2NH_3$

HT These reaction conditions are chosen to produce a **reasonable yield** of ammonia quickly.

Even so, only **some** of the hydrogen and nitrogen react together to form ammonia.

The Haber Process

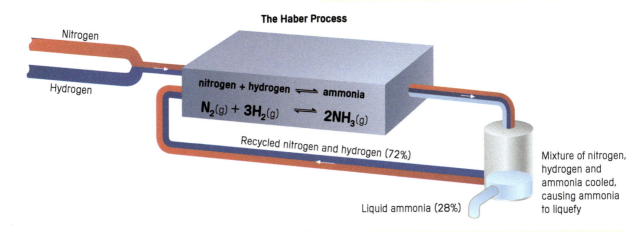

Nitrogen

Hydrogen

nitrogen + hydrogen ⇌ ammonia

$N_2(g) + 3H_2(g) \rightleftharpoons 2NH_3(g)$

Recycled nitrogen and hydrogen (72%)

Liquid ammonia (28%)

Mixture of nitrogen, hydrogen and ammonia cooled, causing ammonia to liquefy

HT Closed Systems

In a **closed system**, no reactants are added and no products are removed. When a reversible reaction occurs in a closed system, an **equilibrium** is achieved when the reactions occur at exactly the same rate in **each direction**. The relative amounts of all the reacting substances at equilibrium depend on the conditions of the reaction.

HT Changing Reaction Conditions

In an **exothermic** reaction…
- if the temperature is **raised**, the **yield decreases**
- if the temperature is **lowered**, the yield **increases**.

In an **endothermic** reaction…
- if the temperature is **raised**, the yield **increases**
- if the temperature is **lowered**, the yield **decreases**.

In **gaseous reactions**, an increase in pressure favours the reaction that produces the least number of molecules.

These factors, together with reaction rates, determine the optimum conditions in industrial processes, e.g. the **Haber process**.

C3 Alcohols, Carboxylic Acids and Esters

Alcohols

Alcohols are carbon-based molecules that contain the **functional group** −OH. Methanol, ethanol and propanol are the first three members of the **homologous series** of alcohols.

Alcohol	Structural Formula	Formula
Methanol	$\begin{array}{c}\quad\quad H\\ \quad\quad |\\ H-C-O-H\\ \quad\quad |\\ \quad\quad H\end{array}$	CH_3OH
Ethanol	$\begin{array}{c}\quad H\quad\; H\\ \quad |\quad\; |\\ H-C-C-O-H\\ \quad |\quad\; |\\ \quad H\quad\; H\end{array}$	CH_3CH_2OH
Propanol	$\begin{array}{c}\; H\quad H\quad H\\ \; |\quad\; |\quad\; |\\ H-C-C-C-O-H\\ \; |\quad\; |\quad\; |\\ \; H\quad H\quad H\end{array}$	$CH_3CH_2CH_2OH$

Alcohols...
- dissolve in water to form neutral solutions
- react with sodium to produce hydrogen
- burn in air
- are used as fuels and **solvents**.

Alcoholic drinks contain ethanol. Ethanol can be **oxidised** to ethanoic acid either by chemical oxidising agents or by **microbial** action.

Ethanoic acid is the main acid in vinegar.

Carboxylic Acids

Carboxylic acids are carbon-based molecules that contain the functional group −COOH.

Carboxylic Acid	Structural Formula	Formula
Methanoic acid	$\begin{array}{c}\quad O\\ \quad ||\\ \quad C\\ H\quad\quad OH\end{array}$	COOH
Ethanoic acid	$\begin{array}{c}\; H\quad\quad O\\ \; |\quad\quad ||\\ H-C-C\\ \; |\quad\quad\;\; \\ \; H\quad\quad O-H\end{array}$	CH_3COOH
Propanoic acid	$\begin{array}{c}\; H\quad H\quad O\\ \; |\quad\; |\quad\; ||\\ H-C-C-C\\ \; |\quad\; |\quad\;\; \\ \; H\quad H\quad O-H\end{array}$	CH_3CH_2COOH

Carboxylic acids...
- dissolve in water to form acidic solutions
- react with carbonates (e.g. sodium carbonate) to produce carbon dioxide
- react with alcohols (in the presence of an acid catalyst) to form esters.

HT Carboxylic acids don't ionise (dissociate) fully in water, so they are called weak acids.

Aqueous solutions of weak acids have a higher pH than aqueous solutions of strong acids with the same concentration.

Key Words   Functional group • Homologous series • Solvent • Oxidised • Microbial

Esters

Alcohols and carboxylic acids react together to form **esters**. When ethanol and ethanoic acid react together the ester formed is ethyl ethanoate.

Esters contain the functional group –COO as shown below:

Ethyl ethanoate (CH₃COOC₂H₅)

Functional group

$$H-\overset{\overset{\displaystyle H}{|}}{\underset{\underset{\displaystyle H}{|}}{C}}-\overset{\overset{\displaystyle O}{||}}{C}-O-\overset{\overset{\displaystyle H}{|}}{\underset{\underset{\displaystyle H}{|}}{C}}-\overset{\overset{\displaystyle H}{|}}{\underset{\underset{\displaystyle H}{|}}{C}}-H$$

Esters are **volatile** compounds (meaning they have a low boiling point).

They have distinctive smells, so are used in perfumes and as flavourings in food.

Quick Test

1. What are the raw materials in the Haber process?
2. What catalyst is used in the Haber process?
3. In the manufacture of ammonia, what temperature and pressure is used?
4. What functional group do all alcohols contain?
5. Which of the following statements is incorrect?
   a) Alcohols dissolve in water to form a neutral solution.
   b) Alcohols react with sodium to produce carbon dioxide.
   c) Alcohols burn in air.
6. What is the name of the carboxylic acid shown below?

$$H-\overset{\overset{\displaystyle H}{|}}{\underset{\underset{\displaystyle H}{|}}{C}}-C\overset{\displaystyle O}{\underset{\displaystyle O-H}{<}}$$

7. Give one use of esters.

1 This question is about elements in Group 1 and Group 7.

a) What name is given to the group of metals in the Periodic Table that contains lithium?

.... **(1 mark)**

b) At the end of each of the statements below state whether they are true or false.

i) Alkali metals have low melting points that increase as you go down

the group. .... **(1 mark)**

ii) Alkali metals are less dense than water. .... **(1 mark)**

iii) Alkali metals become more reactive as you go down the group. .... **(1 mark)**

iv) Lithium fluoride will be a white solid .... **(1 mark)**

v) Lithium fluoride will be insoluble in water .... **(1 mark)**

c) Fluorine is the most reactive element in Group 7. It reacts with sodium chloride as shown below:

fluorine + sodium chloride ⟶ sodium fluoride + chlorine

What type of reaction is this?

.... **(1 mark)**

2 An energy level diagram for a reaction is shown below.

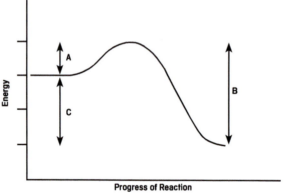

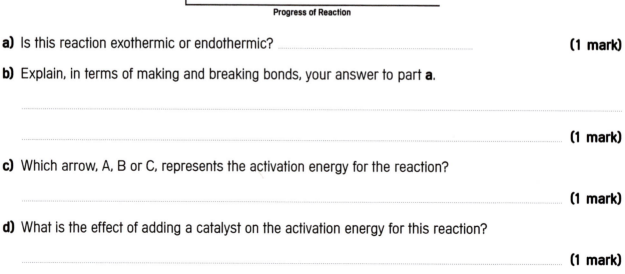

a) Is this reaction exothermic or endothermic? .... **(1 mark)**

b) Explain, in terms of making and breaking bonds, your answer to part **a**.

....

.... **(1 mark)**

c) Which arrow, A, B or C, represents the activation energy for the reaction?

.... **(1 mark)**

d) What is the effect of adding a catalyst on the activation energy for this reaction?

.... **(1 mark)**

3 Ammonia gas (NH_3) is formed by the Haber process. The equation for the reaction is shown below:

$$N_2(g) + 3H_2(g) \rightleftharpoons 2NH_3(g)$$

a) What is meant by the $\rightleftharpoons$ symbol?

.... **(1 mark)**

b) What temperature is used in the Haber process?

.... **(1 mark)**

c) The production of ammonia is exothermic. What is the effect on the yield of ammonia if the temperature is increased?

.... **(1 mark)**

d) What pressure is used in the Haber process?

.... **(1 mark)**

e) State one use of ammonia.

.... **(1 mark)**

4 A student was carrying out a titration to determine the concentration of a solution of sodium hydroxide. She placed 25cm³ of sodium hydroxide into a conical flask and added five drops of indicator. She then carried out the titration using 1mol dm⁻³ hydrochloric acid. The volume of hydrochloric acid used was 22.50cm³.

The equation for the reaction is shown below:

$$NaOH + HCl \longrightarrow NaCl + H_2O$$

a) What piece of apparatus was used to add the acid to the sodium hydroxide?

.... **(1 mark)**

b) Why was an indicator added?

.... **(1 mark)**

c) The number of moles of hydrochloric acid reacting in this titration was 0.0225. How many moles of sodium hydroxide reacted? Explain your answer.

....

.... **(2 marks)**

d) Calculate the concentration of the sodium hydroxide solution.

Use the equation: Concentration of solution = $\dfrac{\text{Number of moles of solute}}{\text{Volume of solution}}$

.... **(1 mark)**

P3 Medical Applications of Physics

X-rays

X-rays...
- form part of the **electromagnetic spectrum**
- have very short wavelengths of the same order of magnitude as the diameter of atoms and can cause **ionisation**
- are used in hospitals to diagnose and treat some medical conditions, e.g. bone fractures, dental problems, Computerised Tomography (CT) scans
- affect a photographic film in the same way as light
- can be detected using **charge-coupled devices (CCDs)** to form an image electronically.

The advantages for medical applications include:
- X-rays are transmitted by healthy tissue.
- X-rays are absorbed by metal and bone to produce shadow pictures.

CT scans produce two- and three-dimensional images. Although significantly more detail is obtained in CT images this is at a cost of increased levels of radiation dose to the patient.

Adequate protective screening, protective clothing and personal radiation detectors are used to monitor and limit exposure.

Ultrasound

Ultrasound are sound waves of frequencies greater than 20 000 Hz, i.e. beyond the upper limit of the hearing range for humans. Ultrasound waves are non-ionising

Electronic systems produce electrical oscillations, which are used to generate ultrasonic waves.

As ultrasonic waves pass from one medium or substance into another, they are partially reflected at the boundary. The time taken for these reflections is a measure of how far away the boundary is.

The distance between boundaries or interfaces can be determined by the equation:

$$s = v \times t$$

where s is the distance in metres (m), v is the speed in metres per second (m/s) and t is half the time taken for the pulse to leave the source, reflect off the boundary and return to the detector

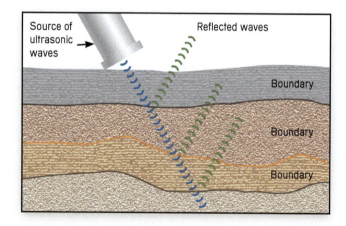

Ultrasound has many uses. Its uses in medicine include...
- pre-natal scanning
- imaging of damaged ligaments and muscles
- imaging of kidneys and destruction of kidney stones.

Reflection of Light

When light strikes a reflective surface it changes direction. This is called **reflection**.

The normal line is constructed perpendicular to the reflecting surface at the point of incidence. For reflected light the **angle of incidence (i)** is the same as the **angle of reflection (r)**.

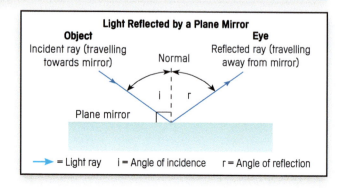

Key Words   X-ray • CCD • Ultrasound • Reflection • Angle of incidence (i) • Angle of reflection (r)

Refraction of Light

When light crosses an interface (a boundary between two transparent media of different densities) it changes direction. This is called **refraction**. No refraction occurs when the light enters the interface at 90°, i.e. along the normal.

The **refractive index** is a property of transparent media and can be determined using the equation:

$$\text{Refractive Index} = \frac{\sin i}{\sin r}$$ where *sin i* and *sin r* are the sine values of the **angles** of **incidence** and **refraction**.

The refractive index of air is 1.0, water is 1.33 and glass is 1.5.

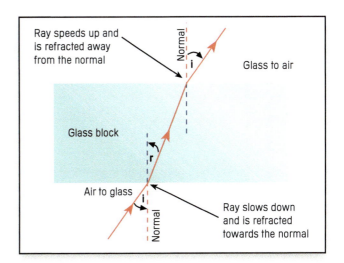

Ray speeds up and is refracted away from the normal

Glass to air

Glass block

Air to glass

Ray slows down and is refracted towards the normal

Converging and Diverging Lenses

A lens is a specially shaped piece of transparent material that refracts light to form an image. There are principally two types of lenses:

- **Converging lens** (**convex lens**) – thickest at the centre and represented by ↕ in ray diagrams.
- **Diverging lens** (**concave lens**) – thinnest at the centre and represented by ⥮ in ray diagrams.

The shape of the lens determines its **curvature**, i.e. how much a light ray is refracted through it. A light ray that enters a lens at its centre is undeviated. This line is called the **principal axis** of the lens.

In a convex lens light from an object is refracted **inwards** at the two curved surfaces of the lens so that they meet at a point called the **focus** or **focal point** (F). This is on the **opposite** side of the lens to the object and is **real**.

In a concave lens the focus appears to come from a point on the **same** side as the object and is not real, i.e. **virtual**.

The distance between the centre of the lens and the focus (real or virtual) is called the **focal length** (f). For **parallel rays** of light the focal point lies on the **principal axis**.

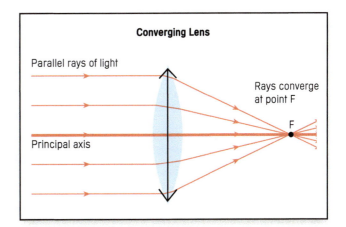

Converging Lens

Parallel rays of light

Rays converge at point F

Principal axis

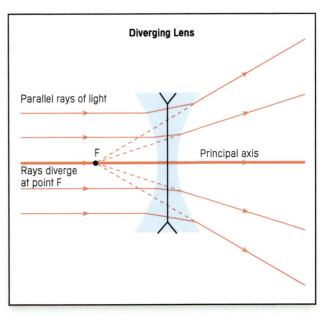

Diverging Lens

Parallel rays of light

F

Principal axis

Rays diverge at point F

Images Produced by Lenses

A lens forms an image by refracting light. The size of an image produced by a convex or concave lens depends on the distance of the object from the lens.

Convex Lens	Concave Lens
The image produced by a convex lens is… • **real** (on the other side of the lens) • **inverted** • **smaller** (for distant objects) or **magnified** (when the object is between 'F' and '2F').	The image produced by a concave lens is… • **virtual** (on the same side as the object) • **upright** (not inverted).

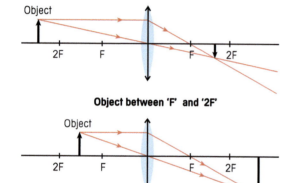

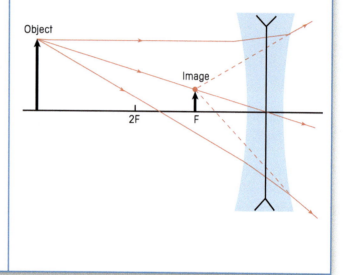

Magnification and Focal Length

The **magnification** of a lens can be calculated using the equation:

$$\text{Magnification} = \frac{\text{Image height}}{\text{Object height}}$$

The magnification of a lens has no units, i.e. it is just a number. A converging lens can be used as a magnifying glass.

The focal length of a lens is determined by…
• the **refractive index** of the material from which the lens is made
• the **curvature** of the two surfaces of the lens.

HT For a given focal length, the greater the refractive index the flatter the lens (i.e. thinner).

Quick Test

1. Name two ways in which X-rays can be detected.
2. Give two examples of ultrasound used in medicine.
3. What is the name given to the phenomenon when light enters a converging or diverging lens to form an image?
4. If the image height is 4.2cm and the object height only 0.7cm, calculate the magnification of the lens.

The Structure of the Eye

The eye receives light and sends this information to the brain via the optic nerve, which interprets the image. The main components of the eye are shown in the diagram.

The **cornea** refracts most of the light whilst the **pupil** (opening in the **iris**) adjusts the light intensity. The **lens** provides further refraction before the image is formed on the light-sensitive **retina**. The **optic nerve** carries this information to the brain.

The **ciliary muscles** control the shape of the eye lens. This allows light from objects at different distances to be brought into focus.

The eye can focus on objects between the **near point** (approximately 25cm) and the **far point** (infinity).

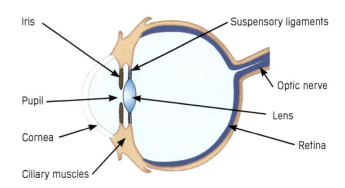

Eye Defects

There are two types of defective vision:
*   **Long sight** caused by the eyeball being too short and unable to focus on near objects.
*   **Short sight**, caused by the eyeball being too long and unable to focus on distant objects.

Both long sight and short sight can be corrected by using **lenses**, which adjust the light before entering the eye to allow it to focus correctly. Spectacles (glasses) are made from concave lenses, convex lenses or a combination of both lenses.

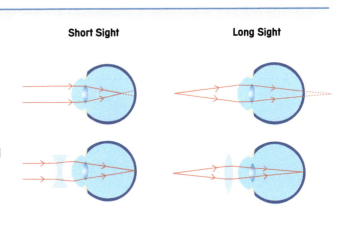

Camera and Magnifying Glass

Unlike the eye, both a **camera** and a **magnifying** glass have **fixed converging lenses** with definite focal lengths.

A magnifying glass enlarges an object size if the distance from the object to the lens is less than the focal length. The image is...
*   **virtual**
*   **upright**
*   **enlarged**.

A converging lens in a camera produces an image on film or via a CCD. These are equivalent to the retina in the eye.

A convex lens magnifies when the object is between the focal point 'F' and the centre of the lens.

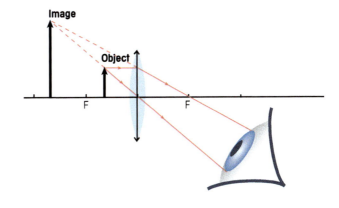

P3 Medical Applications of Physics

Power of a Lens

The **power of a lens** is determined by its focal length using the equation:

$$P = \frac{1}{f}$$

where P is the power in dioptres (D) and f is the focal length in metres (m)

The power of a...
- **converging lens** is **positive** (real focal point)
- **diverging lens** is **negative** (virtual focal point).

The Critical Angle

There are two special cases involving the refraction of light, which occur in two instances:

1 The angle of refraction is equal to 90°. The light ray travels on the boundary between glass and air. The angle of incidence is then called the **critical angle** (c).

HT The critical angle can also be used to determine the refractive index using the equation:

$$\text{Refractive index} = \frac{1}{\sin c}$$

2 The angle of incidence is greater than the critical angle. In this case **total internal reflection** takes place. No refraction occurs so no light escapes from the glass.

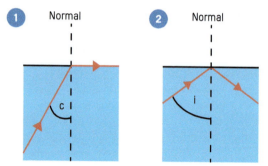

Medical **endoscopes** use the principle of total internal reflection to 'see' inside the body. Visible light is sent down thin, flexible glass rods, called **optical fibres** that are inserted into the body. The image is returned along the same fibres to an eye-piece or camera.

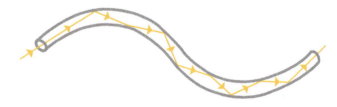

Lasers

A **laser** is a device that amplifies light to produce a very **intense** and very **narrow** beam. The word 'laser' means Light Amplification by Stimulated Emission of Radiation. Lasers can be made from solids, liquids or gases. Modern **devices** are very **small** and **compact**.

Lasers are used in **eye surgery**, for example...
- to repair damaged retinas
- to **remove diseased or damaged cells** by **cutting**, **cauterising** or **burning** the tissue.

Optical fibres are used to guide the laser beam to the correct area of the body.

Quick Test

1 What action do the ciliary muscles have within the eye?

2 What is the normal range of vision of the human eye?

3 What is meant by 'critical angle'?

4 'Total internal reflection' is used in optical fibres. What is total internal reflection?

5 Give an example of where total internal reflection has been applied.

Key Words   Power of a lens • Critical angle • Total internal reflection • Optical fibre • Laser

Centre of Mass

The **centre of mass** of an object is the point through which the **whole mass** of the **object** is considered to act. It can be thought of as the point where all the mass is concentrated.

For example, if you balance an object on the end of your finger, the centre of mass of the object is the point at which the object **balances**. The centre of mass of **symmetrical objects** is found easily by finding the intersection of the **axes of symmetry**.

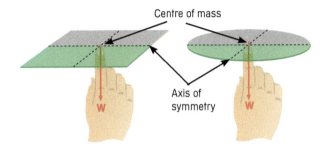

Centre of mass

Axis of symmetry

For thin, irregular shaped materials, with no lines of symmetry, the centre of mass can be found by using a simple plumb line. A suspended object will always come to rest with its centre of mass directly **below** the point of suspension.

Objects with a wide base and a low centre of mass, e.g. Bunsen burners, are more stable than those objects with a narrow base and a high centre of mass, e.g. ladders.

The following method can be used:

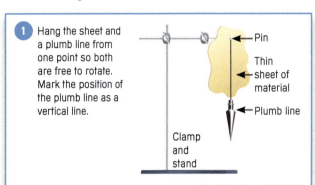

1. Hang the sheet and a plumb line from one point so both are free to rotate. Mark the position of the plumb line as a vertical line.

Pin

Thin sheet of material

Plumb line

Clamp and stand

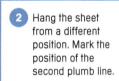

2. Hang the sheet from a different position. Mark the position of the second plumb line.

3. The centre of mass is the point **where the two lines cross**. Check this by balancing the sheet on the end of your finger.

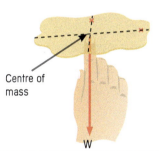

Centre of mass

W

The Pendulum

A mass at the end of a piece of string that oscillates (swings) back and forth is an example of a simple pendulum. The number of times the mass swings back and forth every second gives its **frequency** of oscillation.

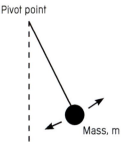

Pivot point

Mass, m

For a simple pendulum there is a connection between the time period and frequency given by:

$$T = \frac{1}{f}$$

where T is the time period in seconds (s) and f is the frequency in hertz (Hz)

The **time period**, T, only depends on the **length** of the pendulum and not on the mass.

Simple applications of this effect are seen in children's **playground rides** and in **fairgrounds**.

P3 Using Physics to Make Things Work

Moments

Forces can be used to turn objects about a particular point – the **pivot point**. The turning effect of such a force is called the moment.

You can calculate the size of a moment by using the formula:

> **M = F × d**
>
> where *M* is the moment of the force in newton-metres (Nm), *F* is the force in newtons (N) and *d* is the perpendicular distance from the line of action of the force to the pivot in metres (m)

You can increase the size of the moment in two ways:

- **Increase** the value of the **force**.
- **Increase** the perpendicular **distance**.

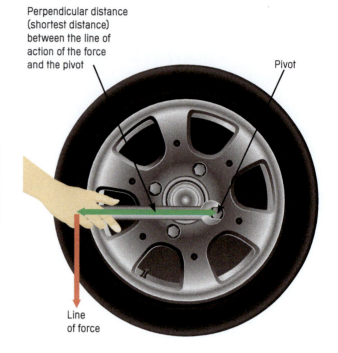

Perpendicular distance (shortest distance) between the line of action of the force and the pivot

Pivot

Line of force

Levers

A lever is a device that acts like a **force multiplier** or a distance multiplier. For example, doubling the length of the spanner to undo a wheel nut will either ...

- double the moment of the force for the same force applied
- allow half the force to be applied to maintain the same moment of the force.

The application of levers is numerous, but two examples include...

- lifting a wheelbarrow
- opening a tin of paint with a screwdriver.

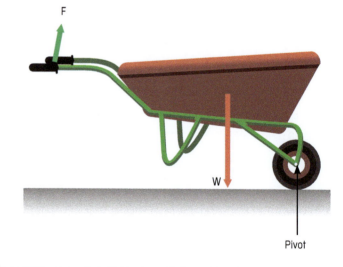

F

W

Pivot

Law of Moments

When an object isn't turning, there must be a balance between...

- the **total moments** of the forces turning the object in a **clockwise direction**
- the **total moments** of the forces turning the object in an **anticlockwise direction**.

This can be shown as:

> **Total clockwise moments** = **Total anticlockwise moments**

This is called the law of moments.

HT Law of Moments

A plank is pivoted at its centre of mass and has two forces F_1 and F_2 pulling it downwards. The plank is balanced and not turning, so the total clockwise moment must equal the total anticlockwise moment.

$$F_1 \times d_1 = F_2 \times d_2$$

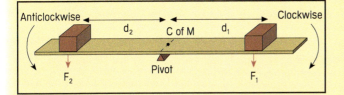

Example

A plank is pivoted at its centre of mass and has balanced forces acting. Calculate F_2.

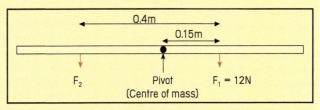

Total clockwise moments = Total anticlockwise moments

$$12N \times 0.15m = F_2 \times (0.4 - 0.15)m$$

$$12N \times 0.15m = F_2 \times 0.25m$$

$$\text{So, } F_2 = \frac{12N \times 0.15m}{0.25m}$$

$$= \mathbf{7.2N}$$

HT Stability

An object will **topple** (fall over) if the **line of action of the force**, e.g. its **weight** lies **outside its base**. The **weight** of the object causes a **turning effect**, which makes the object topple.

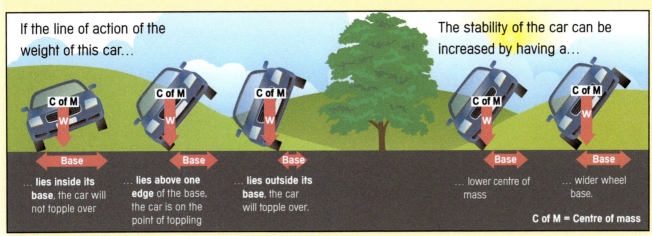

If the line of action of the weight of this car…

…lies inside its base, the car will not topple over

… lies above one edge of the base, the car is on the point of toppling

… lies outside its base, the car will topple over.

The stability of the car can be increased by having a…

… lower centre of mass

… wider wheel base.

C of M = Centre of mass

Quick Test

1. What does the centre of mass represent?
2. What is the position of the centre of mass of a rectangle 5cm long by 3cm wide?
3. An object has forces applied to it but it is not turning. What can be said about the moments on the object?
4. What happens when the line of action of the weight of a car lies outside its base?

P3 Using Physics to Make Things Work

Pressure

Pressure is the **force** that acts over a particular **surface area**. A force acting over a small area gives a larger pressure than the same force acting over a bigger area.

The formula for pressure is:

$$P = \frac{F}{A}$$

where P is the pressure in pascals (Pa), F is the force in newtons (N) and A is the cross-sectional area in metres squared (m^2).

1 Pa is the same as $1N / m^2$

Hydraulic Systems

Liquids are virtually **incompressible**, and the **pressure** in a liquid is transmitted **equally** in **all directions**. This means that a force exerted at one point on a liquid will be transmitted to other points in the liquid.

The pressure in a **liquid** can be used to **work machinery** and is known as **hydraulics**. The effort and load on either side of a hydraulic system can be altered by using different cross-sectional areas. This enables the system to be used as a force multiplier.

Gas

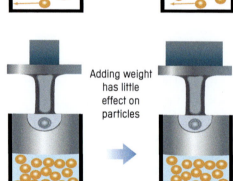

Adding weight compresses gas particles

Liquid

Adding weight has little effect on particles

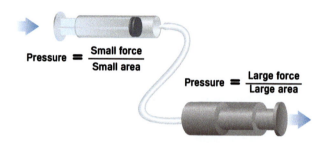

$$\text{Pressure} = \frac{\text{Small force}}{\text{Small area}}$$

$$\text{Pressure} = \frac{\text{Large force}}{\text{Large area}}$$

This idea is used in hydraulic jacks, car braking systems and in mechanical diggers, where a small force is magnified to produce a much larger force at the critical point.

Motion in a Circle

Many objects move in circular, or near circular paths. For example…

- a conker spun on a piece of string
- spinning rides in fairgrounds
- the London Eye
- cars going around corners
- spin driers in washing machines
- satellites orbiting the Earth
- planets orbiting the Sun.

Key Words   **Pressure • Incompressible • Hydraulics**

Centripetal Force

Any object moving with a constant speed in a circular path is **continuously accelerating** towards the centre of the circle.

When there is a change in **velocity** there is an **associated acceleration**. This is because the **direction** of motion is continuously **changing**, not the speed.

The resultant force causing this acceleration is called the centripetal force. This force is always **directed towards the centre of the circle**, i.e. inwards.

The centripetal force may be provided by…
- friction, e.g. a car's wheels on the road surface as the car is turning
- tension, e.g. a conker spun on a piece of string.

The centripetal force needed to make an object perform circular motion increases by…
- **increasing the mass** of the object
- **increasing the speed** of the object
- **decreasing the radius** of the circle.

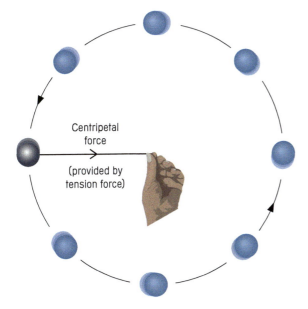

Centripetal force

(provided by tension force)

Quick Test

1. What is the unit of pressure?
2. What is used to transmit the force in a hydraulic system?
3. An athlete is undergoing rotational movement just before he throws a hammer. What provides the centripetal force causing the hammer to accelerate in this way?
4. In circular motion at constant speed why is there a centripetal acceleration?

The Motor Effect

When a current flows through a wire a **magnetic field** is produced around the wire. This **electromagnetic effect** is used…

- on cranes for lifting iron and steel
- in circuit breakers
- in loudspeakers
- in electric bells.

When a wire (conductor) carrying a current is placed in an **external magnetic field**, the **magnetic field formed around the wire** interacts with this permanent magnetic field. This causes the **wire** to experience a force that makes it **move**. This is called the motor effect.

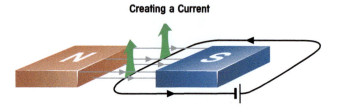

Creating a Current

But, the wire will **not experience a force** if it's **parallel** to the **magnetic field**.

The size of the force on the wire can be increased by…

- **increasing the size of the current** (e.g. having more cells)

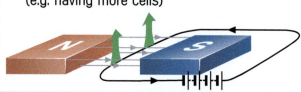

- **increasing the strength** of the **magnetic field** (e.g. having stronger magnets).

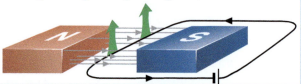

The direction of the force on the wire can be reversed by…

- reversing the **direction of flow** of the current (e.g. turning the cell around)

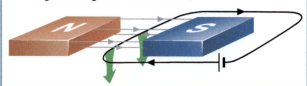

- reversing the **direction of the magnetic field** (e.g. swapping the magnets around).

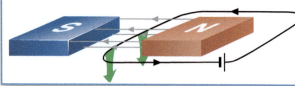

Fleming's Left-hand Rule

The direction of the force can be identified using Fleming's left-hand rule:

- The **F**irst finger points in the direction of the magnetic **F**ield.
- The se**C**ond finger points in the direction of the **C**urrent.
- The thu**M**b points in the direction of the **M**ovement.

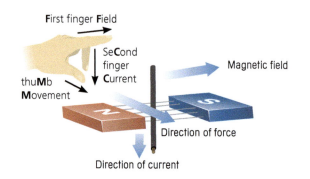

First finger **F**ield

se**C**ond finger **C**urrent

thu**M**b **M**ovement

Magnetic field

Direction of force

Direction of current

Electromagnetic Induction

Electromagnetic induction uses **movement** to produce a **current**. Generators use this effect to produce electricity.

If a conducting wire, or coil of wires, is moved through or 'cuts' through a magnetic field, a potential difference (p.d.) is induced across the ends of the wire. If the coil of wire forms part of a complete circuit, an electrical current will be induced.

If there is no movement, then no current flows.

The same effect is obtained if the coil of wire is stationary and the magnetic field is moved. We call this current an **induced** current.

Induced currents are used in a bicycle dynamo.

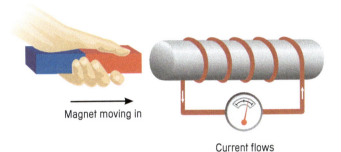

Magnet moving in

Current flows

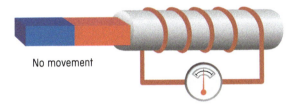

No movement

No current

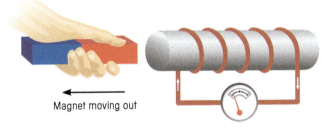

Magnet moving out

Current flows opposite way

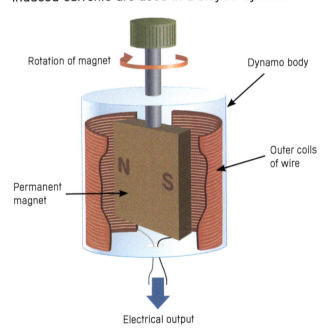

Rotation of magnet

Dynamo body

Outer coils of wire

Permanent magnet

N S

Electrical output

Potential Difference

The size of the potential difference, and hence the current, can be increased by…

- increasing the **speed** of the **movement** of the magnet or coils
- increasing the **strength** of the **magnetic field**
- increasing the **number of turns** on the coil.

Quick Test

1. **a)** What is produced when a current flows through a wire in an external magnetic field?
   b) Give two examples of where this effect has been applied.
2. A loop of conducting wire carrying a current crosses an external magnetic field at 90°. What effect is observed?
3. Briefly describe Fleming's left-hand rule.

Transformers

A **transformer** changes electrical energy from one potential difference to another potential difference. Transformers are made up of two coils, called the **primary** and **secondary coils**, wrapped around a soft iron core.

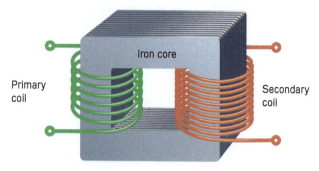

Primary coil

Iron core

Secondary coil

An **alternating potential difference** across the primary coil causes an **alternating current** to flow (input). This alternating current creates a continuously changing magnetic field in the iron core, which induces an **alternating potential difference** across the ends of the secondary coil (output).

The **potential difference** across the primary and secondary coils of a transformer are related by the equation:

$$\frac{V_p}{V_s} = \frac{n_p}{n_s}$$

where V_p is the potential difference across the primary coil in volts (V), V_s is the potential difference across the secondary coil in volts (V), n_p is the number of turns on the primary coil and n_s is the number of turns on the secondary coil

For example, a transformer has 200 turns on the primary coil and 800 turns on the secondary coil. If a potential difference of 230V is applied to the primary coil, the potential difference across the secondary coil can be determined using the equation above.

$$\frac{230}{V_s} = \frac{200}{800}$$

$$V_s = \textbf{920V}$$

Step-up and Step-down Transformers

A **step-up transformer** has more turns in the secondary coil than the primary coil. The potential difference across the secondary coil is **greater** than that across the primary coil.

A **step-down transformer** has fewer turns in the secondary coil than the primary coil. The potential difference across the secondary coil is less than that across the primary coil.

Step-up and step-down transformers are used in the **National Grid** to ensure the efficient transmission of electricity.

A Step-up Transformer

Iron core

Primary coil 200 turns

Secondary coil 1000 turns

A Step-down Transformer

Iron core

Primary coil 1000 turns

Secondary coil 200 turns

Transforming Efficiency

If transformers were assumed to be 100% efficient, the electrical power output would equal the electrical power input (see power, p40). This can be stated using the equation:

$$V_p \times I_p = V_s \times I_s$$

where V_p is the potential difference across the primary coil in volts (V),
I_p is the current in the primary coil in amperes (amps, A),
V_s is the potential difference across the secondary coil in volts (V)
I_s is the current in the secondary coil in amperes (amps, A)

Switch Mode Transformers

Switch mode transformers are much lighter and smaller than traditional transformers and operate at a much **higher frequency**, often between **50kHz and 200kHz**. They operate using the 50Hz mains supply.

Switch mode transformers use very little power when they are switched on, as no load is applied.

They have found useful applications as chargers for…

- **mobile phones**
- **digital cameras**
- **computer laptops**.

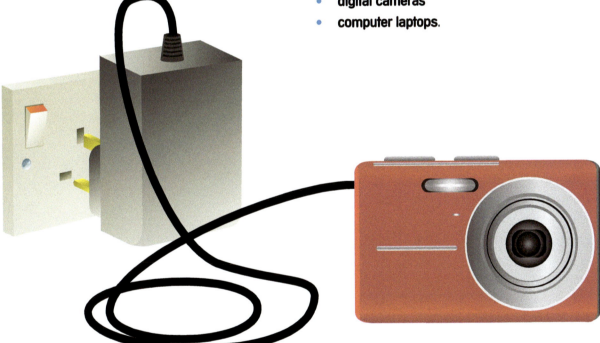

Quick Test

1. What are the main components of a transformer?
2. Do transformers use a direct current or an alternating current?
3. Give two advantages of switch mode transformers over traditional transformers.
4. Over what frequency range do switch mode transformers work?
5. Give an example of the application of switch mode transformers.

1 There are two main eye defects, know as short sighted and long sighted, which can be readily corrected.

a) **i)** Briefly describe the condition of a person who is long sighted.

....

.... **(1 mark)**

ii) This condition is caused by a lack of movement in the eye lens. What controls the shape of the eye lens?

....

.... **(1 mark)**

b) On the diagram below draw two light rays, from the common point shown just in front of the eye, one above and one below the dashed line given, to show the effects of a person who is long sighted.

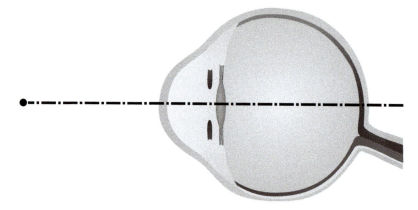

(3 marks)

c) To correct this eye defect a lens can be placed in front of the eye.

i) What type of lens is used to correct for long sight?... **(1 mark)**

ii) What effect does the additional lens have in correcting this defect?

.... **(1 mark)**

d) On the diagram below draw two light rays from the common point in front of the eye to show the effects of using the lens illustrated.

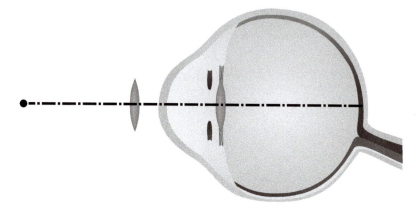

(3 marks)

2 The diagram below shows a coil of wire located between the poles of a magnet.

The arrows indicate the direction of the conventional current.

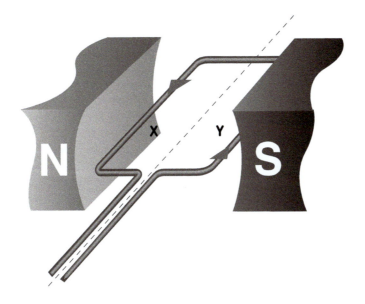

a) On the diagram draw arrows to show the direction of the force on sides **X** and **Y** on the coil of wire. **(2 marks)**

b) What rule is used to determine this direction?

.... **(1 mark)**

c) Explain why these forces cause the coil to rotate.

....

.... **(2 marks)**

d) What is the name given to this effect?

.... **(1 mark)**

e) What would happen to the coil if the magnets were swapped around?

.... **(1 mark)**

f) What two methods could be used to allow the coil to rotate faster about its axle?

....

.... **(2 marks)**

Answers

Quick Test Answers

Page 13
1. Water
2. Energy
3. By active transport and diffusion
4. **a)** Villi
   b) Alveoli
5. **Accept one from:** Large surface area; Being thin; Having an efficient blood supply; Being ventilated

Page 15
1. Moves up and out
2. In the alveoli (air sacs)
3. Transpiration
4. Guard cells

Page 17
1. Right atrium
2. Arteries
3. Valves
4. Muscle
5. White blood cells
6. No nucleus; Contains haemoglobin
7. Phloem
8. Thick walls made from muscle and elastic fibres

Page 20
1. The thermoregulatory centre
2. Pancreas
3. Broken down amino acids
4. In the bladder
5. Dialysis machine
6. Rejection by the recipient's immune system

Page 23
1. Exponentially
2. Farming; Quarrying; Building; Dumping waste
3. Acid rain
4. **Accept one from:** For timber; For land for farming
5. It increases. Because there are less trees, less carbon dioxide is absorbed from the atmosphere during photosynthesis

Page 25
1. Fermentation
2. Methane
3. **Accept two from:** Increased number of cattle and rice fields; more wood being burned; deforestation; more fossil fuels being burned
4. Fungus
5. Increasing the mesh size of nets; Increasing quotas of other types of fish

Exam Practice Answers
1. **a)** The concentration of the sugar solution
   b) **Accept one from:** Temperature; Volume of solution; Time; Size of potato chip (length and width)
   c) 0
   d) Water moves from the sugar solution into the potato by osmosis
   e) Repeat the investigation and calculate a mean
2. Active transport requires more energy; Active transport moves substances against a concentration gradient
3. A massive surface area for exchanging materials (villi); An extensive network of blood capillaries
4. **a)** A – Trachea; B – Bronchus; C – Bronchioles; D – Alveoli
   b) i) Carbon dioxide
      ii) Oxygen
5. giving off water vapour; absorbing carbon dioxide; giving off oxygen
6. lungs; vein; body; deoxygenated
7. Xylem
8. **a)** Deforestation
   b) **Accept one from:** Increased release of CO_2 into the atmosphere; Reduced rate of CO_2 removed from the atmosphere by photosynthesis; Increased amount of methane added to the atmosphere; Reduction in biodiversity; Soil loss; Loss of genetic diversity; Changes in rain pattern; Compaction of soil; Less photosynthesis
9. Fermentation
10. **a)** more concentrated and darker in colour
    b) Glucose; Protein

C3

Quick Test Answers

Page 31
1. In terms of their atomic mass
2. In order of atomic number
3. Hydrogen
4. **a)** higher; harder; less
   b) displace

Page 36
1. Scum
2. Joules
3. It's released
4. Lithium
5. White
6. Copper(II)
7. White

Page 38
1. A titration
2. Litmus
3. $0.75 mol\,dm^{-3}$

Page 41
1. Nitrogen and hydrogen
2. Iron
3. $450^{\circ}C$ and 200 atmospheres
4. −OH
5. b)
6. Ethanoic acid
7. **Accept one from:** Perfumes; Food flavourings

Exam Practice Answers

1. **a)** Alkali metals
   b) **i)** False
   ii) True
   iii) True
   iv) True
   v) False
   c) Displacement / Redox
2. **a)** Exothermic
   b) More energy is released in making new bonds than is used in breaking the bonds in the reactants
   c) A
   d) The activation energy is lowered
3. **a)** Reversible reaction (or equilibrium)
   b) $450^{\circ}C$
   c) The yield (amount) of ammonia decreases
   d) 200 atmospheres
   e) **Accept one from:** Manufacture of nitric acid; Manufacture of fertilisers
4. **a)** Burette
   b) To know when neutralisation has occurred / The end-point has been reached
   c) 0.0225; The NaOH and HCl react in a 1 to 1 ratio
   d) $0.9 mol\,dm^{-3}$

Answers

Quick Test Answers

Page 46
1. Photographic film; CCD
2. **Any two from:** Pre-natal scanning; Imaging damaged ligaments and muscles; Imaging kidneys; Removal of kidney stones
3. Refraction
4. Six

Page 48
1. They control/change the shape of the lens
2. 25cm to infinity
3. The angle of refraction is directed along the boundary or at 90° to the normal
4. When a ray of light remains within a material by repeated reflection
5. In medical endoscopes

Page 51
1. A point at which all the mass is said to be concentrated
2. (2.5cm, 1.5cm) from any corner, or along the axes of symmetry
3. Total clockwise moment = Total anticlockwise moment
4. The car will topple over

Page 53
1. Pa or N/m^2
2. Liquids
3. The tension in the wire
4. The velocity of the object changes because its direction changes and acceleration is the rate of change of velocity.

Page 54
1. **a)** A magnetic field is produced around the wire
   b) **Any two from:** Cranes for lifting iron; Circuit breakers; Electric bell; Loudspeaker; Electric relay
2. The wire experiences a force and moves
3. Thumb points in the direction of the movement, first finger points in the direction of the magnetic field, second finger points in direction of the current

Page 57
1. Soft iron core; Two coils (primary and secondary)
2. Alternating current
3. They are lighter; They are smaller
4. 50kHz to 200kHz
5. **Any one from:** Mobile phone chargers; Digital camera chargers; Laptop chargers

Exam Practice Answers
1. **a)** **i)** It is the inability to focus on near objects
   ii) The ciliary muscles
   b)

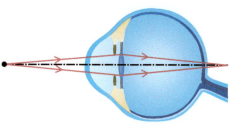

Two light rays must be drawn from the common point; They must show refraction at the lens; They must focus beyond the retina
   c) **i)** A converging lens or convex lens
   ii) It refracts the light before it enters the eye
   d)

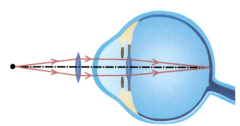

Addition of a convex lens; Light rays showing refraction; Light rays focused on retina
2. **a)** Arrows should be drawn showing that side X moves up and side Y moves down
   b) Fleming's left-hand rule
   c) The coil of wire is on a spindle and the forces produce a moment or turning force; This makes the coil rotate about the spindle axle
   d) The motor effect
   e) The direction of motion would be reversed
   f) **Any two from:** Increase the size of the current; Increase the strength of the magnetic field; More turns

Acid rain – rain with a low pH (acidic) due to the gases released by burning fossil fuels

Activation energy – the minimum amount of energy required to cause a reaction

Active transport – the movement of substances against a concentration gradient; requires energy

Aerobic – with oxygen

Alkali metal – one of the six metals in Group 1 of the Periodic Table

Alternating current (a.c.) – an electric current that reverses its direction of flow repeatedly

Alveoli – air sacs in the lungs; oxygen diffuses out of them and carbon dioxide diffuses into them

Anaerobic respiration – respiration that takes place without oxygen

Angle of incidence (i) – the angle between a ray falling on a plane surface and the normal line at that point

Angle of reflection (r) – the angle between a reflected ray leaving a plane surface and the normal line at that point

Antibody – a protein produced in the body by the immune system to kill particular pathogens

Antigen – a substance that triggers the production of antibodies

Atom – the smallest part of an element that can enter into a chemical reaction

Atomic number – the number of protons in an atom

Atria (singular Atrium) – the upper chambers of the heart

Bacteria – a single-celled microorganism that has no nucleus

Bias – where results are influenced unfairly by an individual's beliefs or opinions

Biodiversity – the variety among living organisms and the ecosystems in which they live

Biofuel – fuel obtained from biomass

Biogas – fuel produced from the anaerobic decomposition of organic waste

Biomass – amount of biological material; the mass of a plant or animal without the water content

Calorie – a unit of energy

Catalyst – a substance that increases the rate of a chemical reaction without being changed itself

Centre of mass – the point at which an object's mass is apparently concentrated

Centripetal force – the external force required to make an object follow a circular path at constant speed

Charge-coupled device (CCD) – a type of microchip that converts light into an electrical signal that is then used to form an image

Ciliary muscles – group of muscles in the eye that control the size of the lens

Concentration gradient – a change in the concentration of a substance from one region to another

Converging (convex) lens – a lens in which light rays passing through it are refracted towards a central point

Critical angle – the angle of incidence that refracts a ray of light at 90° to the normal

Deforestation – the destruction of forests by cutting down large areas of trees

Dialysis – the artificial removal of urea and excess material from the blood (used when the kidneys fail)

Diffusion – the mixing of two substances through the natural movement of their particles from a high concentration to a low concentration

Dilate – to widen or enlarge

Direct current (d.c) – an electric current that flows in one direction

Distillation – a process of separating a liquid mixture by boiling it and condensing its vapours

Diverging (concave) lens – a lens in which light rays passing through it are refracted away from a virtual central point

Efficiency – the energy output expressed as a percentage of energy input

Electron – a negatively charged subatomic particle that orbits the nucleus

Electromagnetic induction – the induced current in a wire as it moves through a magnetic field

Electronic structure – the arrangement of electrons around the nucleus of an atom

Glossary

Element – a substance that consists of only one type of atom

Emulsion – a mixture of oil and water

Endothermic – a reaction that takes in heat from its surroundings

Energy – the ability to do work; measured in joules (J)

Enlarged – bigger than original size

Environment – the area and conditions in which an organism lives

Ester – organic compound containing the functional group –COO

Exothermic – a reaction that gives out heat to its surroundings

Exponentially – with fast growth

Extinct – a species that has died out

Fermentation – the conversion of sugar to alcohol and carbon dioxide using yeast

Fleming's left-hand rule – shows the connection between the directions of magnetic field, current and movement

Focal length – the distance between the lens centre and the focal point along the principal axis

Focus – any point through which rays of light converge

Food miles – refers to the distance food has to travel from where it is grown to where it is sold

Fractional distillation – the process used to separate crude oil into groups of hydrocarbons whose molecules have a similar number of carbon atoms

Frequency – the number of cycles or oscillations that occur in 1 second; measured in hertz (Hz)

Friction – a resistive force acting between two surfaces

Fuel – a substance that releases heat or energy when combined with oxygen

Functional group – the group of atoms in a compound that determines the chemical behaviour of the compound

Global warming – the increase in the average temperature on Earth due to a rise in the levels of greenhouse gases in the atmosphere

Greenhouse effect – the process by which the Earth is kept warm, by the greenhouse gases reflecting heat back to Earth

Guard cells – pairs of sausage-shaped plant cells that open and close to allow carbon dioxide into the leaf and water and oxygen out (through the stomata)

Halogen – one of the five non-metals in Group 7 of the Periodic Table

Haemoglobin – the red pigment in red blood cells, that carries oxygen to the organs

Herbicide – a toxic substance used to destroy unwanted vegetation

Homeostasis – keeping internal conditions of the body constant

Homologous series – a series of organic compounds with the same general formula that have similar chemical properties

Hydraulics – mechanical systems involving the use of incompressible liquids or fluids

Immune system – the body's defence system against infections and diseases (consists of white blood cells and antibodies)

Incompressible – applied to liquids and fluids where the internal forces are the same throughout the substance

Insoluble – a substance that will not dissolve in a solvent

Insulin – a hormone produced by the pancreas that is used to regulate blood sugar levels

Ion – a charged particle formed when an atom gains or loses electrons

Ionic compound – a compound formed when two (or more) elements bond ionically

Ionising power – the ability of particles or electromagnetic radiation to ionise other neutral atoms or molecules

Joule (J) – a unit of energy

Laser – light amplification by stimulated emission of radiation

Law of moments – when the total clockwise motion and total anticlockwise motion of an object are equal

Lever – a simple device that provides mechanical advantage of movement

Long sight – the inability of the eye to focus on near objects

Magnification – the ratio of image size (height) over object size (height)

Methane – a clear gas given off by animal waste; can be used as a fuel; a greenhouse gas

Microbial – relating to microbes

Moment – a turning force; the product of the force and the perpendicular distance from the force to the pivot point

Momentum – a fundamental quantity that is a measure of the state of motion of an object; product of mass and velocity; p = m x v; units of kg m/s

Motor effect – the movement of a conducting wire in a magnetic field

Mycoprotein – a protein-rich food produced from fungi

National Grid – a network of power lines and cables that carries electricity from the power station to the consumer

Neutralisation – a reaction between an acid and a base that forms a neutral solution (i.e. pH 7)

Neutralise – to form a neutral solution

Neutron – a subatomic particle found in the nucleus of an atom that has no charge

Non-renewable – energy sources that can't be replaced in a lifetime

Normal line – the line constructed at 90° to the reflecting surface at the point of incidence

Optical fibre – a thin strand of glass or plastic that uses total internal reflection to carry light

Osmosis – the movement of water through a partially permeable membrane into a solution with lower water concentration

Oxidised – a substance that gained oxygen and / or lost electrons

Oxyhaemoglobin – the combination of oxygen and haemoglobin

Partially permeable – a barrier that allows only certain substances through

Peat – a partially decayed vegetation used for fuel and fertiliser by gardeners

Pesticide – a substance used for destroying insects or other pests

Phloem – tissue for transporting sugars around a plant

Photosynthesis – the chemical process that uses light energy to produce glucose in green plants

Plasma – the clear fluid part of blood that contains various dissolved substances such as proteins and mineral ions

Pollution – the contamination of an environment, e.g. by chemicals or water

Potential difference – the energy transfer by unit charge passing from one point to another; measured in volts (V)

Power of a lens – a measure of the ability of a lens to refract light; $P = \dfrac{1}{\text{focal length}}$

Precipitate – an insoluble solid formed in a precipitation reaction

Pressure – force per unit area; $P = \dfrac{F}{A}$; units of Pascals (Pa)

Principal axis – the line passing through the centre of a lens

Proton – a positively charged subatomic particle found in the nucleus

Reflection – a change in direction of a wave when striking a plane surface

Refraction – the change in direction (and speed) of a wave as it passes from one medium to another

Refractive index – a measure of the ability of a material to refract light given by the ratio of the sine values of the angles of incidence and refraction; also given by $\dfrac{1}{\sin(\text{critical angle})}$

Relative atomic mass (A_r) – the average mass of an atom of an element compared with a twelfth of the mass of a carbon atom.

Relative formula mass (M_r) – the sum of the atomic masses of all atoms in a molecule

Reversible reaction – a reaction in which products can react to re-form the original reactants

Salt – the product of a chemical reaction between a base and an acid

Glossary

Sequestered – the storage of a substance in a solid material through biological or physical processes (e.g. carbon dioxide from the air in bodies of water)

Short sight – the inability of the eye to focus on distant objects

Solvent – the substance that dissolves the solute

Sound wave – forward and backward vibrations within a material or medium; sound waves are longitudinal waves; can't travel through a vacuum

Specialised – adapted for a particular purpose

Stent – a tube inserted into a blood vessel to keep it open

Stomata – openings / pores in leaves

Surface area – the external area of a living thing

Sustainable – resources that can be replaced or maintained in sufficient quantities to support current and future needs

Switch mode transformer – a small, light transformer that operates at frequencies between 50kHz and 200kHz

Tension – a resistive force in a wire or string

Thermoregulatory centre – the part of the brain responsible for maintaining a constant body temperature in warm-blooded animals

Titration – a method used to find the concentration of an acid or alkali

Total internal reflection – the internal reflection of light achieved when the angle of incidence is greater than the critical angle

Transformer – an electrical device used to change the voltage or potential difference of alternating currents

Transpiration – the movement of water through a plant from root to leaf

Type 1 diabetes – a condition where not enough insulin is produced by the pancreas

Ultrasound – high frequency sound waves beyond the range of human hearing, i.e. 20 000Hz

Upright – an image that has the same orientation as the object

Urea – a waste product of protein breakdown formed in the liver and excreted in urine

Urine – water and waste products filtered by the kidneys

Ventilation – the process of breathing in and out

Ventricles – the lower two chambers of the heart

Villi – projections that stick out from the walls of the small intestine; each villus contains a network of blood capillaries for absorbing soluble food

Virtual – an image from which the light rays appear to come from the object

X-ray – electromagnetic radiation of shorter wavelength than ultraviolet radiation

Xylem – tissue for transporting water and minerals in plants

Yeast – a single-celled fungus; a microorganism

Yield – the amount of a product obtained from a reaction

HT **Equilibrium** – the state in which a chemical reaction proceeds at the same rate as its reverse reaction (the reactants are balanced)

Glucagon – hormone made in the pancreas when blood glucose levels fall too low

Notes

1. Reactivity Series of Metals

Potassium	most reactive
Sodium	
Calcium	
Magnesium	
Aluminium	
Carbon	
Zinc	
Iron	
Tin	
Lead	
Hydrogen	
Copper	
Silver	
Gold	
Platinum	least reactive

(elements in italics, though non-metals, have been included for comparison)

2. Formulae of Some Common Ions

Positive ions		Negative ions	
Name	**Formula**	**Name**	**Formula**
Hydrogen	H^+	Chloride	Cl^-
Sodium	Na^+	Bromide	Br^-
Silver	Ag^+	Fluoride	F^-
Potassium	K^+	Iodide	I^-
Lithium	Li^+	Hydroxide	OH^-
Ammonium	NH_4^+	Nitrate	NO_3^-
Barium	Ba^{2+}	Oxide	O^{2-}
Calcium	Ca^{2+}	Sulfide	S^{2-}
Copper(II)	Cu^{2+}	Sulfate	SO_4^{2-}
Magnesium	Mg^{2+}	Carbonate	CO_3^{2-}
Zinc	Zn^{2+}		
Lead	Pb^{2+}		
Iron(II)	Fe^{2+}		
Iron(III)	Fe^{3+}		
Aluminium	Al^{3+}		

Key

| relative atomic mass |
| **atomic symbol** |
| name |
| atomic (proton) number |

| 1 | | **H** hydrogen 1 | | | | | |

Periodic Table (relative atomic mass, **symbol**, name, atomic number):

Group 1	Group 2		Group 3	Group 4	Group 5	Group 6	Group 7	Group 0
								4 **He** helium 2
7 **Li** lithium 3	9 **Be** beryllium 4		11 **B** boron 5	12 **C** carbon 6	14 **N** nitrogen 7	16 **O** oxygen 8	19 **F** fluorine 9	20 **Ne** neon 10
23 **Na** sodium 11	24 **Mg** magnesium 12		27 **Al** aluminium 13	28 **Si** silicon 14	31 **P** phosphorus 15	32 **S** sulfur 16	35.5 **Cl** chlorine 17	40 **Ar** argon 18
39 **K** potassium 19	40 **Ca** calcium 20	(transition metals)	70 **Ga** gallium 31	73 **Ge** germanium 32	75 **As** arsenic 33	79 **Se** selenium 34	80 **Br** bromine 35	84 **Kr** krypton 36
85 **Rb** rubidium 37	88 **Sr** strontium 38	(transition metals)	115 **In** indium 49	119 **Sn** tin 50	122 **Sb** antimony 51	128 **Te** tellurium 52	127 **I** iodine 53	131 **Xe** xenon 54
133 **Cs** caesium 55	137 **Ba** barium 56	(transition metals)	204 **Tl** thallium 81	207 **Pb** lead 82	209 **Bi** bismuth 83	[209] **Po** polonium 84	[210] **At** astatine 85	[222] **Rn** radon 86
[223] **Fr** francium 87	[226] **Ra** radium 88	(transition metals)						

Transition metals block:

45 **Sc** scandium 21	48 **Ti** titanium 22	51 **V** vanadium 23	52 **Cr** chromium 24	55 **Mn** manganese 25	56 **Fe** iron 26	59 **Co** cobalt 27	59 **Ni** nickel 28	63.5 **Cu** copper 29	65 **Zn** zinc 30
89 **Y** yttrium 39	91 **Zr** zirconium 40	93 **Nb** niobium 41	96 **Mo** molybdenum 42	[98] **Tc** technetium 43	101 **Ru** ruthenium 44	103 **Rh** rhodium 45	106 **Pd** palladium 46	108 **Ag** silver 47	112 **Cd** cadmium 48
139 **La*** lanthanum 57	178 **Hf** hafnium 72	181 **Ta** tantalum 73	184 **W** tungsten 74	186 **Re** rhenium 75	190 **Os** osmium 76	192 **Ir** iridium 77	195 **Pt** platinum 78	197 **Au** gold 79	201 **Hg** mercury 80
[227] **Ac*** actinium 89	[261] **Rf** rutherfordium 104	[262] **Db** dubnium 105	[266] **Sg** seaborgium 106	[264] **Bh** bohrium 107	[277] **Hs** hassium 108	[268] **Mt** meitnerium 109	[271] **Ds** darmstadtium 110	[272] **Rg** roentgenium 111	

Elements with atomic numbers 112–116 have been reported but not fully authenticated

*The Lanthanides (atomic numbers 58–71) and the Actinides (atomic numbers 90–103) have been omitted.

Cu and **Cl** have not been rounded to the nearest whole number.

$s = v \times t$	**s** distance **v** speed **t** time
refractive index $= \dfrac{\sin i}{\sin r}$	**i** angle of incidence **r** angle of refraction
magnification $= \dfrac{\text{image height}}{\text{object height}}$	
$P = \dfrac{1}{f}$	**P** power **f** focal length
HT refractive index $= \dfrac{1}{\sin c}$	**c** critical angle
$T = \dfrac{1}{f}$	**T** periodic time **f** frequency
$M = F \times d$	**M** moment of the force **F** force **A** cross-sectional area
$P = \dfrac{F}{A}$	**P** pressure **F** force **A** cross-sectional area
$\dfrac{V_p}{V_s} = \dfrac{n_p}{n_s}$	V_p potential difference across the primary coil V_s potential difference across the secondary coil n_p number of turns on the primary coil n_s number of turns on the secondary coil
$V_p \times I_p = V_s \times I_s$	V_p potential difference across the primary coil I_p current in the primary coil V_s potential difference across the secondary coil I_s current in the secondary coil

Index